Bound to the Hearth by the Shortest Tether

Village Life in China, Brazil, and Points in Between

Paul Chandler

UNIVERSITY PRESS OF AMERICA,® INC.

Lanham • Boulder • New York • Toronto • Oxford

Copyright © 2006 by
University Press of America,® Inc.
4501 Forbes Boulevard
Suite 200
Lanham, Maryland 20706
UPA Acquisitions Department (301) 459-3366

PO Box 317
Oxford
OX2 9RU, UK

Library of Congress Control Number: 2005933775
ISBN 0-7618-3332-3 (paperback : alk. ppr.)

For Mary

Contents

List of Maps

List of Tables

Acknowledgments

During the course of conducting the research upon which this book is based as well as during its writing, I have accumulated many debts. Grants and scholarships were received from three sources. The Ball State University Center for International Programs funded my exploration for research opportunities on Costa Rica's Talamanca Reserve. Indiana Partners of the Americas funded a similar venture to the Kaïngang Reserves of Rio Grande do Sul in Brazil. And the Committee for the International Exchange of Scholars— Fulbright Commission supported my efforts in Minas Gerais in Brazil.

Nanjing Forestry University in China and the Federal University of Viçosa in Brazil each hosted me while I pursued my research and tolerated my presence with great patience. To the good people of the village of Lijiayang in Fujian Province, China, especially the family of Mr. Wu Zaiyuan, I owe much for their willingness to permit me to live and work among them. To the good people of the village of Prudentes in Minas Gerais, Brazil, especially the family of Sr. Eduardo dos Reis, I am indebted for their hospitality, friendship and good humor.

To two gentlemen in China, Dr. Hsiung Wenyue, Professor of Bamboo Ecology at Nanjing Forestry University, Mr. Liu Maosong of the Kengdi Village Committee, and Mr. Nathan Ye of Jinling Vocational University in Nanjing, I am grateful for their courage and skill in arranging the conditions that allowed me to enter and reside in Lijiayang. To two gentlemen in Brazil, Dr. Laércio Couto, Professor of Agroforestry at the Federal University of Viçosa, and Sr. Sebastian Araújo de Oliveira I am grateful for their introductions and patience while working in Prudentes.

I am thankful to Ms Kirsten Huffman of Dunkirk, Indiana, and Sr. Carlos Baldetti of Guatemala City, Guatemala, for their review of early drafts of this work and their encouragement to see it through to the end.

To two gentlemen, Dr. Morris Sun and Sr. Bartolomeu Romualdo, who served as field assistants and offered me their dedication, hard work, invaluable advice, and irreplaceable friendship, I owe a debt that can never be repaid.

Finally, and most importantly, I owe the greatest of debts to Mary for bringing me the peace of mind and the knowledge of love that liberated me to focus on the task of putting on to paper a lifetime of curiosity, inquiry and work for others to share.

Where I have erred, the blame is mine alone.

INTRODUCTION

Chapter One

The Worldwide Disappearance
of the Rural Villager

A few years back the opportunity came for a first, and so far only visit to England. Among many places, this was one I had most longed to visit. This desire had come through discovering *England*, a book containing Edwin Smith's full-page black-and-white photographs[1] in my grandfather's library. For this trip, between a few days in London and the eventual destination of Oxford, I traveled through Devon, Cornwall and Somerset. The tour to see for myself, in color, the book's beauty spots met my best expectations. However, while winding my American-sized rent-a-car through the narrow roads of this corner of England I encountered the local form of a worldwide phenomenon. It should not have been unexpected.

Rural England, like rural areas throughout the world, was in the midst of a thorough transformation. The first indicators were the virtual absence of cattle in these three counties and the "For Sale" signs on the gates of many small farmsteads. While sheep could be seen on the moors, the only cattle seen during that week were a few head enclosed in a single small pasture. Later, a sign on a pasture fence beside another ancient farmhouse answered the question raised by the many unseen cattle. It advised all who read it that the pasture was under quarantine, a result of the epidemic hoof-and-mouth disease that had passed through these counties two years earlier.

This transformation of southwestern England mirrored that of my old home. Rural producers, unable any longer to make a living had given up and sold their land or were in the process of doing so. In rural England, just as in rural North Carolina, the buyers were urbanites in search of retirement homes, second homes, investments in real estate, a realized fantasy of the country estate, or the recapture of an imagined simplicity within village life. Along my route through rural England new Jaguars were more common in the drives of homes than old farm vehicles. The rural-to-urban exodus of the impoverished and dispossessed begun with Britain's industrialization had been succeeded by an urban-to-rural land rush enjoyed by the more prosperous of the many beneficiaries of an urban, post-industrial, and global economy.

Economists may see this at least seasonal urban-to-rural migration as the result of agricultural production efficiency and urban prosperity in the wealthier nations of the world, but the rural people who have called their villages home for generations are more likely to see it as the end of a sometimes hard, but always meaningful life. Rural villagers in less wealthy nations such as Brazil or China often share that view, even without the rural expressions of urban wealth in an England or the "New South" of the United States.

In China rural transformation came first as villages were drawn from feudal subsistence to dead end local spurs of the market economy during the earlier paleo-imperial days of globalization. After the Second World War, much of the best that remained of traditional social and ecological order in China's villages was lost during Chairman Mao's cataclysmic campaigns to eradicate the last bit of the worst that also remained. Now, with the all-but-unbelievable economic growth wrought by reforms initiated a generation ago by the late Deng Xiaoping, rural China may yet see village life become the good life.

In Brazil rural transformation has come not from the end of a communist command economy, but fitfully by the repetitive boom-and-bust of that nation's elitist, technocratic, have-and-have-not corporate capitalism. More recently, more subtly, and perhaps more significantly, another transformation is being marked by the growth of new avenues for expressions of faith. In contrast to rural China, feudal traditions linger in rural Brazil, often with the blessing of local, increasingly itinerate religious authorities. These traditions, though undertaken with the best of motives, work to keep many of the poorest of its rural villagers dependent on the few remaining local land-owning elites.

In China and Brazil more than ancient ways of life on the land are being lost. This volume is an attempt to preserve a small bit of what is disappearing from the world's countryside along with its rural people. To the degree that it achieves its purpose, this book may serve students and academics interested in ethnographic methods, rural societies, Asian or Latin American studies, or that infinitely varied and so infinitely defined class of humans called peasants. This book may also inform and serve the rural traveler, armchair, professional and otherwise. The more curious will learn what the author has learned about how rural people survive and in some cases prosper, how their villages organize and divide themselves in the process, and what tends toward good results. The more studious will learn how the author learned these things, and perhaps how they might learn something of a similar nature. And the more adventurous will learn how important both planning and preparation, as well as luck and serendipity, are to the successful pursuit of ideas, arguably either profound or esoteric, to unarguably isolated locales.

Part 1 of this volume describes the pursuit of indigenous ecological knowledge developed around China's *shamu jianzhong*, the world's oldest known system of timber management. The original study was designed to assess the validity of the local ecological knowledge underlying the management system. It sought to identify where the local knowledge was and was not isomorphic with published ecological knowledge derived through research and practice by university and government scientists over the past half-century. It opens with a discussion of the natural and human history of the forested highlands of south China before turning to the trials of first accessing and then residing and working in a pair of rural villages in the mountains of Fujian Province. Beyond the anticipated findings of the research, one of the ethnographic by-products includes an unanticipated insight into the role rights to real property can play and, in the villages, are hoped to play in the ultimate liberation of China's rural producers. This part concludes with accounts of unique aspects of Chinese culture manifested in the course of my time in country.

Following Part 1, a brief detour into a crowded field is indulged. This recounts explorations of several indigenous regions of Central and South America for their potential to support any adventures in curiosity more convenient, and fundable, than China to a North American academic. This detour marks a change in research focus as it outlines how many indigenous American populations have become overworked, quasi-professional academic research subjects while the greater masses of their non-indigenous rural village neighbors attract far less expert curiosity, despite the greater availability of this mass to serve as grist for popular "participatory" trends in rural development and applied anthropology.

Making use of this opportunity, Part 2 investigates those villagers necessarily hidden on the flip side of current participatory methods, the ones who do not participate. It originates with a study of reasons for non-participation in efforts to provide rural assistance to all households within a group of isolated village hamlets in Brazil's inland state of Minas Gerais. As with the first, this second part begins with a discussion of natural and human history, in this case of the "bush zone" of Minas Gerais, and follows with an account of the challenges presented by efforts to realize the study. Collateral experiences along the way illustrate how elitism, particularly among university educated, self-described environmentalists, serves the landed rural haves, increases Brazil's already great socio-economic differentiation, and accelerates the exodus of its landless rural poor, all in the name of protecting the rural environment. It also discusses how a religious transformation occurring throughout Brazil may hold promise for improving the ecology, independence, and self-sufficiency for those hoping to remain part of that country's rural village life. This second part concludes with a discussion of some of the challenges unique to Brazil likely to confront anyone working in its rural villages.

While this book is structured around original research, its greater purpose is to share insights encountered by chance as well as by plan while living among these two rural populations. Beyond the nominally scientific matters, this volume also discusses what is necessary for an outsider to enter into the world of the rural villager and describes a variety of cultural institutions seemingly designed to maximize the likelihood that those attempting to better the rural villager's life are ineffective, if not actually counter-productive in pursuing their goals.

This book is an account of people whom, if not ignored, are more commonly viewed romantically or ideologically rather than realistically and on their own terms. It is unavoidable that this type of work be something of a personal account and thus, of course, subject to both idiosyncratic and egocentric emphases, not to mention failings. As much as this is a description of methods and findings in social science research, it is an account of learning how to learn from rural people, of enduring a small share of the physical, cultural, social and psychological hardships they confront on a daily basis, and of why, despite the frequent futility of much of the effort to better the lives of these people, it is nonetheless an effort well worth undertaking.

NOTES

1. Edwin Smith and Geoffrey Grigson, *England* (New York: The Viking Press, 1961).

Part One

VILLAGE LIFE IN THE
MOUNTAINS OF FUJIAN

Chapter Two

A Brief History of the
Shamu Jianzhong

Shamu, or Chinese-fir (*Cunninghamia lanceolata*) has been the single most important timber species in China for as long as written records of forestry have existed in that country.[1] It also has the world's longest history of management for timber production.[2] Today it is still widely distributed in the fertile valleys and lower slopes of the hilly and mountainous areas of south China at elevations from about 300 to 1800 meters. The work of archaeologists documents the use of *shamu* for coffins and caskets far back into the Zhou Dynasty (11th to 3rd Centuries BCE) and for the walls and furnishings of some tomb chambers of the Western Han Dynasty (206 to 24 BCE).[3] *Shamu* was also the preferred species for shipbuilders at least as far back as the Qin Dynasty (220 to 207 BCE).[4] Other common uses of the wood included house building, furniture, containers, carving, and fuelwood. The bark was widely used as a substitute for terra cotta roof tiles. The reason why *shamu* had such extensive utilization was not only related to its abundance in nature, but also due to the ancient people's recognition of the excellent characteristics of *shamu* timber, of its height, straight stem, thick and bulky bole, durability, straight grain, fine texture, insect resistance, rot and decay resistance, moisture resistance, and great ability to float.[5] About 1200 years ago in southern Zhejiang Province *shamu* also became the focus of what later became the world's oldest known timber scaling system. By early in the Ming Dynasty (1368 to 1644 CE) in the southern Zhejiang village of Longquan a father-and-daughter team systematized this focus and developed the scaling rules adopted as the official standards for *shamu*, known as the *Longquan Majie*. This system estimated timber value based upon a given log's length and wood clarity, but significantly not its diameter.[6] China's historic scarcity of timber and super abundance of human labor effectively eliminated the cost advantages of manufacturing wood products from larger rather than smaller stems of trees.

Cultivation of *shamu* began at least as early as the Eastern Han Dynasty (25 to 220 CE), both for afforestation and courtyard plantings.[7] From the writings of this period it cannot be determined with certainty what type of material was used for planting stock. Greater certainty of the type of planting stock used for afforestation comes later from the work of the Tang Dynasty (618 to 907 CE) poet Bai Zhuyi. His poem "Planting *Sha*" (*Zai Sha*) indicates that the planting stock had roots as the verb *zai* implies that digging was part of the planting process. If unrooted planting stock had been used the verb most likely to have been employed would have been *cha*, "to insert." Some lines from the poem—"transplant before the east window" (*yizai dongquan qian*) and, as Bai apparently did not like to see impressive forest trees rendered into roof laths, "misused mountain seedling" (*weizhi shanshang miao*)—strongly suggest that the planting stock at this time was wildlings, uprooted and transplanted natural seedlings. This poem indicates that this form of *shamu* forest regeneration is at least 1100 years old.[8]

In charting the history of *shamu*, the origin of the use of unrooted cuttings as planting stock is placed either during the Five Dynasties period (907 to 960 CE) or early in the Northern Song Dynasty (960 to 1127 CE).[9] This innovation apparently came in response to the value of *shamu* in both domestic and foreign trade along with the inability of natural regeneration and wildlings to compensate for the already great rates of deforestation occurring in China. *Agriculture and Sericulture Fundamentals* (*Nongsang Jiyao*), published in 1273 CE during the early part of the Yuan (Mongol) Dynasty (1271 to 1386 CE), presents the first recorded mention of cutting afforestation with *shamu*.[10] This document indicates that use of *shamu* cuttings for afforestation is at least 700 years old or, if other estimates are accurate, perhaps over 1000 years old.[11]

Direct seeding of *shamu* was practiced by at least one of the minority nationalities of Guizhou Province in south central China. In his 1749 CE *Account of the Southern Qian* (*Qiannan Shilue*), Ai Bida described how these people selected the seed from the higher, more vigorous branches of phenotypically superior trees, prepared the soil, and then sowed the seed to produce a forest ready for harvest in as few as twenty years.[12] Yu Xintuo, Professor of Forestry at Fujian Forestry University, has also noted that the minority nationality populations of this region have a long history of using coppicing, root-collar cuttings, branch cuttings, wildlings, sprout layering, and even seedlings for regenerating *shamu* forests. Professor Yu's work further documents this part of southeastern Guizhou Province as the only region of China where all six of these methods were known to have been in practice.[13]

Aside from these various forms of regeneration, other aspects of *shamu* management have a history of many centuries in China. Significant among these is what the Chinese call "space planting" (*jianzhong*) or, as it is usually translated, intercropping. Various production systems built around agricultural intercropping of *shamu* had been in practice for millennia across most of the highlands of south China.[14] According to Yu[15] and Menzies,[16] this remained true until the early 1960s, and in more isolated mountainous areas as recently as the late 1970s. In the villages where the original research was undertaken, the last examples were initiated opportunistically on just over a dozen hectares between 1976 and 1979, or during the uncertainties of authority of the Mao-to-Deng transition. The *shamu jianzhong*, the traditional system of agricultural intercropping centered on *shamu*, represents an intermediate form between shifting cultivation and the forms of agricultural intercropping advocated today by both academics and international forestry and resource development agencies.

Shifting cultivation occurs in areas where the population is relatively sparse and at least locally migratory. In relation to the agricultural part of the cycle, the forest plays the role of a fallow or green manure crop to restore soil fertility; to maintain soil structure, texture, and moisture holding capacity; and to provide supplementary tree crops, fuel, and construction materials between the periodic harvests of agricultural crops. The agricultural portion of the cycle is typically counted in years and the forest, or silvicultural, portion in decades.[17] In contrast, modern agroforestry typically employs trees and agricultural crops simultaneously throughout the rotation, with the trees providing supplementary food, fuel, fiber, or construction materials and protection for the agricultural crops against wind and water erosion or other adverse climatic conditions. In some cases agricultural production ceases with the forest plantation's crown closure, then for the remainder of the rotation the site's productive capacity is devoted exclusively to the forest crop.[18] The differences between these systems and the *shamu jianzhong* arise from a combination of economics, biology, history, and land tenure.

A 1636 edition of a gazetteer published in Zhejiang Province estimated the market value of *shamu* to be five times that of alternative cash crops such as ginger, lacquer or charcoal. Other gazetteers published in Hunan and Guizhou Provinces reported double to tenfold return on investments from crops of *shamu*. Market values of this magnitude for *shamu* meant, as Oxford historian Nicholas Menzies wrote, "farmers came to perceive timber as a crop in its own right rather than as a by-product of land clearance or as a secondary product grown to satisfy household needs. . . . The economic opportunities offered by timber crops would have been instrumental in orienting hill farmers toward growing trees rather than undertak[ing] the enormous investment of labour needed to practise terraced, irrigated agriculture."[19]

The role of biology is no less crucial in the *shamu jianzhong*. Just as with redwood, giant sequoia, Japanese sugi, and other members of the Taxodiaceae, or baldcypress family, *shamu* features a trait unique to that family among the conifers: the ability to resprout after cutting. This resprouting occurs from the exposed cambium, root suckers, and dormant root collar buds, each providing a source of planting stock of known phenotypic quality. Also like other members of the Taxodiaceae, *shamu* grows rapidly with good form and remains sound to great age. But unlike most other members of this family, *shamu* is in its early years intolerant of direct sunlight. In fact, without cultivation *shamu* is such a poor competitor in its early stages of growth that stands of natural origin are all but unknown in China today.[20] In its first two to five years, *shamu* needs sufficient shade to maintain higher levels of relative atmospheric humidity and soil moisture and prevent direct insolation of the soil surface above its roots. Once it has established itself and if it has not suffered excessive competition from weeds, *shamu* enters a period of rapid growth that may last for one or two decades or longer.[21] The presence of taller agricultural crops around the *shamu* would provide just the sort of modifications of microclimate it required until the period of rapid growth occurred. The regular tending of agricultural crops would reduce weed competition for the young trees. And the value of the *shamu* timber, if not the value of the agricultural crops themselves, would provide sufficient justification for tending trees through intercropping.

Several historical patterns of land tenure found in pre-1949 China would also facilitate growing *shamu* as a crop. In Fujian this included the prevalence of "Crown land" (*guantian*) that, despite its name, existed largely outside official control. Earlier scattered populations along with newer settlers, both usually of various non-Han ethnic and linguistic traditions, were forced upslope on to this Crown land to gain access to new lands, as most of the best agricultural land in south China had been occupied by Han farmers between the Tang Dynasty and the Southern Song Dynasty (1127 to 1279 CE). One group of newer settlers, known as the "shed people" (*pengmin*) because of the temporary housing their migratory habits required, moved on to the open lands of the mountains, cleared them, and planted a variety of cash crops, including timber.[22] Under these circumstances *shamu* would be an obvious choice for cultivation.

In Fujian Province another common feature of land tenure was absentee landlords. To gain access to land, peasants would often sign contracts with these landlords. The terms of the contracts varied from the "one field two landlords" (*yi tian liang zhu*) system to sharecropping. The one field two landlords system gave the tenant full use rights to the land surface, or "mountain skin" (*shanpi*), and all crops he produced on it in return for an annual rent, while the landlord retained ownership of the "mountain bones" (*shangu*).[23]

The sharecropping contracts were more restrictive and possibly exposed the *shamu jianzhong* system to the ills of detached managerial decision-making by absentee landlords. These contracts often specified the spacing of the *shamu* stand, the intercrops that could cultivated, the frequency of tending for the trees, and the rotation ages of the stand, usually twenty to thirty years. The landlord usually had full rights in the trees and a claim on anywhere from one-third to two-thirds of the food, fiber, medicinal, and oil-bearing intercrops. In return, the peasant had access to land and a chance for himself and his family to survive for a few more years. Increasing population and widespread rural poverty in China made such sharecropping contracts attractive to the peasants.[24]

Precisely when intercropping was introduced into the system of cultivating *shamu* is not known, but Lan,[25] Menzies,[26] and Yu and Sun[27] have all made estimates of its beginnings from a number of ancient writings. In its discussion, *The Best Selection of Crops, Mulberry, Clothing, and Food (Nongsangyishi Cuoyao)*, written during the Yuan Dynasty, made no mention of *shamu* intercropping, but early in the succeeding Ming Dynasty intercropping was discussed in several works. *The Atlas for the Masses' Convenience (Bian Min Tucuan)* and the *All-Flower Guidebook (Qun Fangpu)* both mentioned planting sesame with *shamu* early in the rotation. The former book said that sesame, in addition to providing edible oil, was beneficial to the growth of *shamu* by accelerating the decay of the roots of competing brush and grasses. Later in the Ming Dynasty the *Special Book for Betterment (Zhifu Qishu)* advocated planting millet in the summer and wheat in the winter whenever and wherever the existing forest had been cleared and a stand of *shamu* was to be established. Still later, Xu Guangpi's 1639 *The Complete Book of Agricultural Administration (Nongzheng Quanshu)* provided a detailed instruction for the *shamu jianzhong*.

Where there are extensive mountains and rich soil, first plow the land and sow sesame for a year or more. Then at the beginning of the second month, when the "pneuma" (*qi*) are most abundant, cut sprouts one *chi* (1/3 meter) in length. Use a dibble to make a hole and insert (*cha*) to half its length. Press the soil firmly. . . Do not allow weeds and other vegetation. Weed and hoe every year. . . If the mountain is suitable for growing crops, then sow millet in the summer and wheat in the winter, which can substitute for weeding and hoeing.[28]

The system described by Xu has changed little in the intervening 350 years, but, as will be discussed in a later chapter, those changes are significant. The traditional *shamu jianzhong* system has taken a number of forms. Yu and Sun discussed the system from several aspects.[29] A summary of their description based on "fixed-year limits" is most economical for purposes of explanation:

(1) Cultivate crops first, then plant *shamu*. This is the form Xu Guangpi described and the one that most resembles shifting cultivation. After clearing the forest the site is burned and then for one or two years is planted or sown to agricultural crops before the *shamu* is regenerated. Historically, any of the crops listed in Table 2.1 could be employed in this form of intercropping; however, as noted earlier, in pre-1949 China the choice was often the landowner's prerogative. Due to soil nutrient depletion, the delay of regeneration, and the potential for soil erosion and water loss, Yu and Sun state that this form is most disadvantageous for cultivating *shamu*.

(2) Plant *shamu* first, then cultivate crops. Yu and Sun say this form is rare, occurring only when certain shade-demanding medicinal crops are needed.

(3) Simultaneous planting of *shamu* and cultivation of crops. Lan,[32] Huo,[33] Yang,[34] as well as Yu and Sun all cite this as the most common form

Table 2.1.   *Shamu* Intercrops (adapted from Huo[29] and Yu and Sun[30])

Annual staples	Cash crops
wheat (*Triticum aestivum*)	tobacco (*Nicotiana tabacum*)[b,c]
buckwheat (*Fagopyrum* sp.)	indigo (*Indigofera* spp.)[a]
millet (*Panicum miliaceum*)	ginger (*Zingiber* spp.)
hill (dry) rice (*Oryza sativa* var.)	plantain (*Musa paradisica*)[b]
maize (*Zea mays*)[a,b]	bast ramie (*Boehmeria nivea*)[a]
sorghum (*Sorghum vulgare* var.)[a]	pineapple (*Ananas comosus*)
taro (*Colocasia esculenta*)	cotton (*Gossypium* spp.)
cassava (*Manihot esculenta*)[a,c]	
sweet potato (*Ipomoea batatas*)[b]	Medicinals
lima bean (*Phaseolus limensis*)[b]	Job's tear (*Coix lacryma-jobi*)
string bean (*Vigna sinensis*)	peucedanum (*Peucedanum decursivum*)
long bean (*Vigna cyclindrica*)	zicao (*Lithospermum* spp.)[d]
	dangshen (*Colonopsis pilusila*)[d]
Edible oils	baizhu (*Atractyloides macrocephala*)[d]
soybean (*Glycine max*)	safflower (*Carthamus tintorius*)[d]
peanut (*Arachis hypogaea*)	opium (*Papafer somniferum*)
rapeseed cabbage (*Brassica napus* var.)	
sesame (*Sesamum indicum*)	
tung-oil (*Aleurites fordii*)[c]	
cubeb litsea (*Litsea cubeba*)[a]	

[a]These are considered high-stemmed crops, commonly planted during the first year of intercropping, occasionally in the second, and rarely in the third.
[b]New World crops.
[c]These are also considered high-stemmed crops, but they require more time to mature and bear fruit and so are left in the *shamu* stand for as long as five to ten years.
[d]These medicinal crops are also frequently consumed as vegetables or, in the case of safflower, used for extracting edible oils.

of intercropping in continuing practice. Lan has provided a concise general description:

- Fell all plants in the forest and brushland, then burn and plow the site.
- Plant *shamu* cuttings at a density of about 900 to 1500 stems per hectare.
- Interplant with annual crops and tung-oil.
- During the cycle harvest annual crops in the first three or four years, collect tung-oil seeds from the fourth to seventh years, fell the tung-oil trees in the eighth or ninth year, then ten years later harvest the *shamu*, commonly without performing any intermediate cuttings; that is, the number of stems in the final harvest is the same as the number planted, less any mortality.

This third form is cited as the generally preferable form of intercropping. It provides the most intensive tending for the young stand, minimizes soil and water losses, provides the *shamu* with the protective cover it needs for establishment on and occupation of the site, and, if the intercrops are selected wisely, minimizes the crops' consumption of the soil nutrients the *shamu* needs for growth.[35] In this form the high-stemmed crops (Table 2.1) are usually employed in the first year and the low-stemmed crops in the succeeding two or three years. A variation of this form of intercropping foresters should appreciate, but which is exceedingly rare, occurs where soil conditions are poor and features one or two years of green manure crops turned into the soil for the specific purpose of improving the growth of *shamu*.[36]

Professor Yu has said that intercropping has been practiced wherever traditional forms of *shamu* cultivation have occurred in China, regardless of the local methods of regeneration, and that the first form of intercropping, planting *shamu* after one or two years of cropping, is older and, except among minority nationalities utilizing longer rotation ages, less frequently practiced than the preferred third form.[37]

The *shamu jianzhong* regeneration practices and the systems of intercropping both met the requirements of a long history of traditional practice needed for the original research that took me to China. Both are several centuries old and both show several signs of an apparent evolution of efficiency and productivity. Just as importantly, the *shamu jianzhong* could still be found in its fully traditional forms in the recent living memory, if not in practice, in China in the late 1980s, although as will be discussed in the next chapter, a foreigner was not always personally able to study or view them. Also, as the most historically important timber species in China, *shamu* has been a frequent subject of modern scientific research.

In the late 1980s existing research in China provided readily available explanations of many aspects of the cultivation of *shamu*, especially those related to intercropping. However, China's cultural and political peculiarities inhibited and in some cases even prevented study by both foreigners and the Chinese themselves of some very important aspects of the practices employed in cultivating *shamu*. In addition, changes in forest practices law during the early to mid-1970s and in the forms of land ownership since 1949 had brought the use of the *shamu jianzhong* system to an end in many parts of China where it had enjoyed centuries of practice and development. These problems and peculiarities notwithstanding, the *shamu jianzhong* offered a fully acceptable, perhaps even an optimal, resource management system to test a somewhat unusual hypothesis: The traditionally derived knowledge of ecological processes held by long-term rural practitioners was functionally isomorphic with the knowledge derived through the application of the modern scientific method.

Identifying and accessing a suitable population able to describe the practice of the *shamu jianzhong* from a basis of personal experience proved to be a far greater challenge than identifying a suitable system.

NOTES

1. Yu Xintuo, *Shanmu* (sic) (Fuzhou: Fujian Science and Technology Press, 1983), 1–5 (Chinese).

2. China Woody Plant Flora Committee (CWPFC), *Silvicultural Techniques of China's Main Tree Species* (Beijing: China Forestry Press, 1981), 3–28 (Chinese).

3. Zhao Yi, "A Summary of the History of Cultivating and Utilizing *Shamu*," *Sichuan Forest Science* 2 (April 1980): 85–86 (Chinese).

4. Lan Taigang, *Modern Evaluation of Certain Traditional Shamu Cultivation Measures* (master's thesis, Nanjing Forestry University, 1987), 30 (Chinese).

5. Zhao, "A Summary of the History," 85.

6. Xia Zhennong, ed., *Term Ocean* (Shanghai: Shanghai Dictionary Publisher, 1979), 2–3 (Chinese).

7. See note 4 above.

8. Zhao, "A Summary of the History," 86.

9. See note 4 above.

10. ———, "A Summary of the History," 87.

11. See note 4 above.

12. Claudine Lombard-Salmon, *Un Exemple d'acculturation Chinoise: la Province du Guizhou au XVIIIème Siècle* (Paris: École Française d'Extrême Orient, Vol. LXXXIV, 1972), 127.

13. Yu, *Shanmu*, 6, 100.

14. K.F.S. King, "The History of Agroforestry," in *Agroforestry: A Decade of Development*, eds. Howard A. Stepfler and P.K. Ramachandran (Nairobi: International Council for Research in Agroforestry, 1987), 3–11.

15. Yu, *Shanmu*, 4.

16. Nicholas K. Menzies, "The History of Forestry in China," in *Science and Civilization in China*, ed. Joseph Needham (Cambridge: Cambridge University Press, 1985), 145–147.

17. Ester Boserup, *The Conditions of Agricultural Growth* (New York: Aldine Publishing Company, 1965).

18. See note 14 above.

19. Menzies, *Trees, Fields, and People*, 93–95.

20. Huo Yingchang, "The Effects of Soil Quality and Tree Growth of Burning, Site Preparation, and Intercropping with *Shamu*," *Guangdong Forest Science and Technology* 4 (October 1975): 7–10 (Chinese).

21. Liu Honghe and Wei Zuocheng. "Preliminary Analysis of the Causes of Fast Growth in Young Stands of *Shamu*," *Forest Science and Technology* 7 (July 1985): 13–14 (Chinese).

22. Stephen Averill, "The Shed People and the Opening of the Yangzi (sic) Highlands," *Modern China* 9, no. 1 (January 1983): 84–126.

23. Wu Xiangxiang, "A Compendium of Chinese Popular Customs," *China Historical Collection*, Series 6, Vol. 1 (Taipei: Wenxing Bookshop, 1962): 27–30 (Chinese).

24. Menzies, *Trees, Fields, and People*, 99.

25. See note 4 above.

26. Menzies, *Trees, Fields, and People*, 85–87.

27. Yu Xintuo and Sun Peiling, "Forest Intercropping," in *Shamu*, ed. Wu Zhongren (Beijing: Forestry Press, 1984), 431–441 (Chinese).

28. Zhao, "A Summary of the History," 88.

29. See note 27 above.

30. Huo, "The Effects on Soil Quality and Tree Growth," 8.

31. Yu and Sun, "Forest Intercropping," 435.

32. See note 4 above.

33. See note 20 above.

34. Yang Hanxi, "*Shamu* Forest Management Research," in *Thirty Years of China's Forestry Technology and Science,* ed. Yang Hanxi (Beijing: China Forestry Science Academy of the Scientific Information Institute, 1979), 164–175 (Chinese).

35. See note 20 above.

36. See note 27 above.

37. Yu Xintuo, pers. comm. (President, Fujian Forestry University, January 19, 1988).

Chapter Three

Clan in a "Closed County"

Of the many difficulties faced in the late 1980s by an American graduate student wishing to pursue ethnographic research in rural China, access to a suitable population in "the field" was the most universally opposed by the Chinese. In this case, "the field" was necessarily an isolated and certainly impoverished rural mountain village, the only type of place where traditional forms of the *shamu jianzhong* were likely to exist in living memory, much less in practice.[1] The necessity for a foreigner to live for several months in such a place presented the Chinese with a number of possibilities, all high on their collective list of cultural, political, and personal dislikes. The easiest way for a Chinese to avoid any of these possibilities had the benefit of being, at least to that Chinese, a perfectly reasonable response to any request a foreigner might make to locate, inspect, or identify, much less reside in some village far removed in both time and space from China's urban centers: "It is not permitted." Few sensible reasons why "it is not permitted" were ever explained, and none officially.

Some resistance to the pursuit of this research was expected, but the educational utility of the process of overcoming the resistance was not. Such naïveté had been encouraged back in Seattle by the process of securing an invitation to teach at and conduct research through Nanjing Forestry University, a school with which the University of Washington's College of Forest Resources had an existing exchange relationship. The university president in Nanjing responded to my official inquiry with an offer of a two-year visa, a one-year contract to teach conversational English, and his personal assurance of the university's "assistance in your research conducting."

The situation showed promise. In addition to the assurance of the university's president, a visiting scholar from Nanjing at the College of Forest Resources was encouraging. Her husband, Professor Jiang Zhilin was also a member of the faculty in Nanjing and, as good further fortune seemed to have it, had specialized in agroforestry. Surely Professor Jiang would be an ideal contact for pursuing the indigenous knowledge at work within a traditional agroforest system. Thus buoyed, preparations for two years in China were laid and executed.

"PERHAPS YOU WILL SEE SOMETHING BAD"

The first true lucky break in the search for indigenous knowledge in rural China came on the third day in Nanjing with the self-introductory arrival at my door of Ye Nan, the son of a professor of silviculture in Nanjing. The other foreigners at the university, a German couple, had branded him as "sticky" for his persistence in making contact with anyone who might, at worst, help him practice English and, at best, emigrate to "the West." Like all self-made men, his first step was to make himself useful. He began with advice.

"He has no power." Ye Nan justified his recommendation that I forget Professor Jiang, the only contact I had in Nanjing. Instead, I should make contact with Dr. Hsiung Wenyue. "He has power. If he wants your research to be done, it will be done. He also wishes to become an international professor, so he will want your research to be done" Fortunately, Ye Nan was right. A working but officially retired professor of bamboo ecology, Dr. Hsiung not only wanted the research done, but recommended it be done focusing on the *shamu jianzhong*. Although there was no suitable way to measure Dr. Hsiung's "power," a meeting a few days later followed by a bit of library work indicated the wisdom of the man's recommendation as well as Ye Nan's advice.

"You must do it now!" Ye Nan next insisted that the sincerity of the university's offer of assistance with my "research conducting" must be tested as soon as possible. The means to conduct this test would have another, equally timely purpose. It would be a personal request to the university president for travel permission to search Fujian and Anhui Provinces for suitable study populations in as many poor, isolated rural mountain villages as possible during the long upcoming semester break and New Year's celebration. The university president listened to my request, but answered that he did not believe the university had offered to assist me in my research. Producing the letter over his signature assuring just such assistance brought silence, an obvious blow to the man's "face," and no meaningful change of opinion. Just as Ye Nan had insisted, the offer had not been sincere. And just as Ye Nan had noted, Dr. Hsiung had the power to make the insincerity irrelevant.

His power was not unlimited, however. The situation remained in limbo for several weeks until, without any input from myself, an arrangement was eventually worked out. The worst part was that my wife would have to leave China during my second year as she was not teaching and therefore was not entitled to live in university housing. The best part was that Ye Nan would be my guide and escort during the first part of the search in Fujian. A "young teacher" from the university, a master's student of Professor Jiang, would replace Ye Nan in Anhui. Although this young man was one of my English students, the switch was undertaken for the benefit of Professor Jiang, "so he will not lose face." The possibility that Ye Nan might guide the search in both provinces was ruled out as his father was a departmental colleague of Professor Jiang, which meant that Ye Nan's presence would be seen as a personal as well as professional implication that the young teacher, and hence Professor Jiang, was incompetent to do the job. Accordingly, the plan was to travel to Anhui, but only after concentrating the search in Fujian.

In a few weeks, various interpretations of the entire tale of how the upcoming trip had come about were becoming common knowledge among the students in my four classes, and the tone in all four had changed. With the exception of a few of the sons of rural villages who had taken an interest in my interest in rural villages, including the one tasked to be my escort through Anhui, the students ranged from sullenly cool to vocally hostile to the idea.

"We're tired of western sociologists coming to China and saying, 'Oh! China is poor!'"

"We know there are poor people in America. Why do you have to come to China to live with poor people?"

The fact that these "poor people" might hold knowledge of interest to an American graduate student, perhaps even of utility to China as well, was unimportant. The late Chairman Mao's argument in his "little red book" that the search for useful knowledge was an obligation of "the educated classes" carried no philosophical weight in post-Mao China. That the work would be a theoretical and intellectual challenge was no justification. The idea that it was an adventure was as foolish as the idea that it was "serving the poor." No one reason or combination of reasons compensated for the potential humiliation to these young people that lay in the possibility that "Perhaps you will see something bad" in their China. Sensitivity to their sensitivities did not change the fact that "something bad" to the eyes of an American had already been encountered plenty of times during a few months without leaving Nanjing, or that something good might be seen in an isolated rural village. Neither China's past grandeur nor future promise could negate the reality of today's rural villagers, the embarrassingly poor relations of the nation's best and brightest.

The attitudes of my students reflected an old Chinese saying: "*Laizhe bu shan, shanzhe bu lai.*" What is coming is not good, what is good is not coming.

If actions speak as loudly as words, most of the faculty of Nanjing's English department appeared to hold views similar to those of their students. Smiles became briefer or disappeared altogether. "Pinhead" Li, the professor who taught the writing counterpart to my conversational English course, so known within my apartment to distinguish him from "Sergeant" Li in the university's foreign office, began to use his class time to tell the students that Americans do not speak English well and, more pointedly, that "You should not work with the American." This was easily dismissed as paranoia, envy, or simple backwardness. When personal attacks failed to change the situation, he began to speak ill of the research, of which he knew nothing. When eventually asked to explain his opinion, he could only say, "I don't know anything about your research, but I think it cannot be very important." But that question led him to escalate his hostility. For the remainder of the semester he brought his complaints to the foreign office, to the university president, and even to Dr. Hsiung. The summary that filtered back to me held that the foreigner "does not love China," otherwise he would not be pursuing research that was clearly insulting to China. Dr. Hsiung had the power to ignore all of this, and advised me to do the same.

So, despite students, colleagues, and supervisors, in December Ye Nan and I had "hard seat" tickets on the train to Fujian.

"BUT THIS IS A *REAL* CHINESE NAME!"

While the university's semester break was the only time open to search for a prospective research population, it was a particularly terrible time to travel in China. It seemed as though everyone in the country was going to Fujian for the holidays. Our "hard seats" would have been welcomed as most of the trip was spent standing in the aisle between the rows of wooden benches. The train was so crowded that many had climbed up into the luggage racks above the benches to sleep or at least get off their feet. For us sleep was impossible. Men occasionally fought over seats and babies howled constantly. People chewed on sticks of raw cane and, once the sugar was extracted, either spit the pulp on the floor of the car or, more frequently, just opened their mouths and let the chewed pulp fall where it may. The same process applied to sunflower seeds and roasted peanuts. Eight hours later, by the time the train made it to its second stop in Anqing, the snack droppings covered the floor to a depth of well over half-a-foot. Railroad attendants swept out this first layer with hand brooms, but by Nanchang and later by Nanping new, deeper layers of chewed and shucked crop debris had been deposited. Arrival in Nanping found us both exhausted, but greatly relieved by being off that rolling garbage can.

Although the government Forest Farm at Wangtai had been contacted by Dr. Hsiung and told to expect us, Ye Nan chose Nanping as our first stop so we could visit Fujian Forestry University. There, with any luck, we hoped to find advice on villages where suitably traditional practices of the *shamu jianzhong* could be located. Although it took almost two days, Ye Nan's salesmanship brought us an introduction to Dr. Yu Xintuo, a retired professor and former president of the university.

Professor Yu had literally written the book on *shamu*,[2] and gave us a copy. More importantly, he had several suggestions of where traditional forms of agroforest intercropping with *shamu* were likely to be found in Fujian.[3] As expected, the most promising were far from Fujian's two main valleys and connecting central plateau, but another possibility was not far from Wangtai. So it was back on the train. During this hour-long journey Ye Nan explained that I should avoid speaking any Chinese, as this would encourage those we spoke with to be more open.

"We were delayed," was Ye Nan's seasonally credible reason for our delay. No further questions were asked.

The staff at the Forest Farm gave us a brief drive through the nursery areas and a nearby stand of *shamu*, but hurriedly so as not to be late for the next meal. The mere fact that *shamu* was being grown here according to methods dictated by the national Ministry of Forestry made Wangtai useless for testing the research hypothesis. The educated classes of China took great pride in saying that such matters as forest management were based on science. Using the Forest Farm system of management as the object of study would reveal that the knowledge underlying this system was based on the science used to design it. This would be a hardly remarkable, not to mention foolish, finding.

After I explained all this to him in English, Ye Nan withheld this conclusion. Instead, he informed the Farm staff that unless we were able to find a better location we would have to settle for Wangtai as our site, and unfortunately, with the holiday upon us it will be very difficult to visit other places. Much to my surprise, they put a jeep and driver at our disposal to take us to Taining, the first possibly suitable locale suggested by Professor Yu.

Ye Nan explained the Farm's generosity. "They do not want you to live there. They are afraid that perhaps you will see something bad."

Taining was no more suitable than Wangtai, but for a different reason. "They made much revolution here," Ye Nan explained. In practical terms, that meant that Forest Farm methods were in practice throughout the valley. If any villagers further back in the hills had recently continued or even held living memories of the traditional methods, they would be unwilling to speak of them. A dozen years after his death, Mao's legacy of "political struggle" still held the Chinese mind in its grip.

The trip to Taining was not a waste. Although it was the usual Chinese small town study in grays and browns, there was something in the place that at least made it seem different. First, there were openly visible "free markets". Instead of being tucked back on secondary alleys as in Nanjing, Taining had people selling fresh meats, fresh vegetables, steamed bread dough called *mantou*, and other items unimaginable in the government's public dispensaries. These stalls filled all the alleys adjoining the town's main street, even spilling out a few meters on to the sidewalks in many places. Second, there was the architecture. Nothing fancy, but solid granite block structures closed to the streets but opening into long alleys within. In other parts of China this form of arranging residences is called *hutong*. Each stone archway through the alley marked a different household's domain. Above the main doorway in one, red-painted characters were cut into the stone meaning, "Four generations one roof." And last, the people within each family's domain, most uncharacteristically for the Chinese encountering strangers, smiled as we walked through. In one Ye Nan was finally prompted to ask, "Have you ever seen an American before?"

"Yes!" the man answered proudly. "Just last year there were two. One from France and one from Germany."

With better spirits but poorer means of transportation, we took a bus from Taining to a more southerly county where we hoped to locate a village named Changding. As we rode south, people out for a holiday walk often slowed the bus to a crawl. They strolled three, six, nine, or more abreast along the pavement. At rare moments one or two might look back to see what was making noise behind them, but even this encouraged no one to move aside a millimeter to allow the bus or any other vehicle to pass. Still, because no standing in the aisle was permitted and thus no hawking of cane, peanuts, or other snacks was possible, the bus was marginally better than the train. Ye Nan and I got the last two tickets and squeezed into the last bench, Ye Nan in the corner and me beside a mother and father with an infant still a few months away from his first birthday. With an attentive mother, the child was quiet. An hour or two into the half-day journey the mother sensed her child needed to urinate. As most Chinese infants and toddlers wear split breeches, it was simply a matter of holding the back and knees up and encouraging the child to relieve itself. This she did, but directly over my travel bag.

"*Dui bu qi, tongzhi.*" No offense, comrade.

Eventually we arrived in Changting city, the small seat of government for the county of the same name. Ye Nan asked the first person we met outside the bus station and he directed us to the offices of the Forest Ministry. The people in Wangtai had telephoned the day before to inform them we were coming. Surprisingly, they had another jeep ready and waiting for us. A junior staffer soon appeared. After a brief talk with Ye Nan, punctuated by a laugh over the confusion always created by the similarity of the names Changting and Changding, the young man directed me to sit beside the driver while he and Ye Nan took the back seat.

After the jeep's shallow but steady climb up to a small plateau was found a village of long, wooden homes standing on the flat, brown, hard-packed crest of a broad hill. This was Changding, a study in smoke and mud. Forests stood on other hills far in the gray winter distance. Several meters away men stood smoking as they clutched faded green People's Liberation Army greatcoats about them against the damp chill. Directly in front of the jeep's path a boy of perhaps ten or twelve years stood drooling, barefoot, and ankle-deep in wet brown goo, his filthy pants barely halfway up his thighs, his filthy once-white shirt covered in stains from many sources, and his unnaturally long hands hanging apelike almost to his knees. The isolation and poverty of this nightmare suggested promise as a research site.

Changding held another personal, albeit irrelevant attraction. If one headed due west, not more than a day's walk away over the most distantly visible ridge, he would arrive in Ruijin in Jiangxi Province. This village was Mao's original "revolutionary base area" in the late 1920s. It was from Ruijin that The Long March, made famous to Americans in Edgar Snow's *Red Star over China*,[4] had begun. That book, and the mid-sixties scenes on the evening news of the "little red book" hysteria signaling the advent of the Cultural Revolution, had been the sparks that first lit my interest in China.

Later we were hosted by the local director of the Forest Ministry to a New Year's feast back in their Changting offices. Following the usual pattern, about a dozen other men joined the feast of free food and, since it was New Year's, free drink. We watched the director pick through the plates of common and seasonal foods. "Just like a pig," Ye Nan whispered in English. Before any discussion began, the director hosted several toasts of clear sorghum *gaoliang* whisky. By the fourth or fifth toast he was sloshing *gaoliang* on to Ye Nan's maps and spiral notebook. Ye Nan was increasingly put off by the man's rapidly growing drunkenness.

The problem began when Ye Nan told me to give the director my business card. This card had been prepared in Seattle. My wife had gone to the International District to consult an astrologer for a name better than the usual phonetic transliterations Americans pick for themselves. Mine would have been the moronic Chan Dele, the latter pronounced "*duh-luh*." The name determined by the astrologer was Zeng Wenhua. Zeng, a fairly uncommon, but hardly rare *xing* or family name, implied the relationship between great-grandchildren and great-grandparents. In my case, that would have meant a relationship with dead people. Not promising, except for perhaps a historian. Wenhua, the given name, implied an affection for the "magnificence" that is China.

The director read the name. "But you don't look Chinese." Ye Nan explained that I was not Chinese, that the name had been acquired through an astrologer.

"Oh," the director said, nodding, "your father is Chinese." Ye Nan explained the source of the name again.

The director thought a moment. "Your grandfather is Chinese."

"No," Ye Nan repeated, this time with emphasis. "It's just a name. He purchased it from an astrologer."

While everyone else became silent, the director studied the card in obvious consternation. "But this is a *real* Chinese name!"

"No, no," Ye Nan repeated. "The name is Chinese, but he is American."

Again the director paused, studied the card a bit more, and finally decided. "Oh, oh, now I know! Zeng! Zeng! Your great-grandfather is Chinese."

Ye Nan lost it. "No, no, no!" he shouted. "He is not Chinese! His father is not Chinese! His grandfather is not Chinese! His great-grandfather is not Chinese! He is American! All his family is American! It's just a name he purchased!"

With that outburst the banquet ended immediately and we were back on the road to Wangtai, having no opportunity to ask any villagers about the *shamu jianzhong* and no more encouragement than the potential to question the accuracy of the director's assertion that "only modern methods" were used in his realm.

From Wangtai we took the train to its terminus in Fuzhou, the capital city of Fujian Province. From there the next morning we took a bus up a long climbing road leading gradually away from the coast to Shouning, the seat of a northern county of the same name that had been recommended by Professor Yu. Changding might well have been as suitable as could have been hoped, but the encounter with the director had not been all that was hoped.

Daoist burial tombs could be seen from the road at almost every turn as the bus wound upward through the mountains.

FAMILY IN CHINA

Shouning County on the northern border with Zhejiang Province had been saved for last as it was the most difficult site to reach, a plus for its likely suitability, and entry required a "closed county permit," a much weightier negative for my being able to reside on site. Ye Nan's salesmanship would be tested, but fortunately the peak dissipation period of the New Year's festival had passed.

When the bus arrived shortly before dark, Shouning city revealed itself to be yet another dingy mud hole, but smokier than most. We reported to the Forest Ministry office at a lucky moment. The five members of the junior staff were all dressed in blue Mao suits, mildly liquored up, and playing mahjong. Having an extra man, the loser of each round had to sit under the table during the next round. It promised to go on all night. Ye Nan and I were a brief diversion until we were shown to a bare, dusty room where we would be allowed to sleep on the floor, which proved impossible. The mahjong game in fact continued until dawn when the men had to report for work again. One groggy staffer flagged down a passing tractor, spoke to the driver for a moment, and told Ye Nan the man would take us further up the road to Kengdi to the police station to request a permit.

The tractor was an oversized version of the two-wheel garden tractor some ambitious backyarders in America have, but had a hitch to which a two-wheeled cart was attached. The whole contraption moved like an articulated chassis bus, but more jerkily with its small weight and plow-type handlebars. Plus, it was very cold in Shouning. Ye Nan and I were to stand in the cart and hold on to a bar welded on to the front of the cart's box all the way up the mountain. At the last moment, the staffer ran back into the office and a moment later brought out two of the bulky, green People's Liberation Army great coats before waving at us dismissively as he returned inside.

The situation was not promising. While the police in China take greater pride in their government service than most Chinese, their favorite phrase was the usual "it is not permitted." Judging from Ye Nan's silence and eyes-forward concentration as we bumped along, the actual New Year did not appear to improve things in his mind.

"You do not speak no any Chinese," Ye Nan instructed as we finally climbed stiffly from the cart in front of the police station. The officer at the door was frowning. Silently he led us inside to a brightly lit office. Behind the desk was the station's commander, a lieutenant we judged by the first officer's address, but as was common he wore no bars of rank on his uniform. He was also frowning. Ye Nan sat down and went to work. He was not through his second sentence when the lieutenant interrupted him to ask if we had business cards. We each produced one and Ye Nan's face went gray as he sat back in his chair.

After the earlier business card incident, my thoughts were on names. One tradition among the Chinese is to give children an unfortunate name at birth.

If they survive until their first birthday, they will be given a better name designed to provide what the astrologer believes they will otherwise lack. Zeng, my adopted Chinese *xing*, despite its modification by the love of China implied in my given name, had already caused a problem in China. That *xing* is China's closest equivalent to the Scots' clan was a source of more bitter irony. My clan is Menteith, a minor clan allied to the Stuarts and earlier infamous for having sired the betrayer of William Wallace, the symbol of Scottish independence. It seemed as though some curse made long ago was finally visiting itself on the other side of the globe.

The lieutenant glanced at Ye Nan's card briefly, but gave mine more attention. "Zeng Wenhua, is it?"

"*Dui, dui.*" Yes, yes, we answered in sad unison.

"Are you my cousin?" the lieutenant asked.

I was not sure I understood the word "cousin," but as per his own advice Ye Nan would have translated anyway. "No," he answered glumly. "He is an American."

"But we have the same *xing*," the lieutenant said.

Lieutenant Zeng stood up, extended his hand, and with an enormous smile said, "Welcome back to China."

We were struck dumb, but rose and shook his hand in turn.

"How long will you need to stay?" he asked cheerily. He called for the officer who had shown us in, told him to get the permit book but forget the forms, and pointing to me said, "He is my family. Can you imagine?"

Ye Nan ran with the opportunity presented by this misunderstanding. He grabbed my arm and shook it, "You must speak with him in Chinese! He thinks you are his cousin," he insisted.

"Yes, yes, I am Zeng, Zeng Wenhua," I said, shaking his hand again. "I have come to learn from the peasants," I added.

Lieutenant Zeng waved his free hand dismissively. "No problem. I will prepare all the papers." He took the permit book, waved the first officer away, and turned to Ye Nan. "His Chinese has worsened," he said. Then he began a rapid back-and-forth about my reason for being in here and what it was that we were looking for. "*Ye pian ye hao,*" Ye Nan concluded. The poorer the better.

"Good, good," he nodded as he escorted us out of his office. He spoke to a third officer, relayed the long-lost cousin story again, and shortly we were back outside as the officer brought yet another green government jeep from behind the station. He motioned me into the front seat, Ye Nan into the back, drove us several blocks to a nondescript *hutong*, and soon emerged with a small, elderly, sharp-eyed, and vigorous man in a green Mao suit. He was introduced as Secretary Liu Maosong and it was explained that he would know the best place for our work.

Secretary Liu climbed in back with Ye Nan and directed the policeman driving the jeep to take us to Lijiayang, the "Pear Family Ocean." Smiling broadly, Lieutenant Zeng waved to us as we drove away.

Although we were not certain for another seven months, Lijiayang was, as it looked, perfect for the research (Map 3.1). Intensive annual agriculture occupied all but two of the village's households, which totaled 91 and included 357 persons total.[5] Two kilometers further up the road was a second, smaller village named Linfengkeng, the "Forest Wind Spring," with another 21 households and 104 people,[6] all intensive cultivators and all members of the Shezu, a tiny ethnic "minority nationality" whose language, rather than Sino-Tibetan as with Han, had originated from the Yao-Miao language family of northern Indo-China.[7] Both villages engaged in irrigated terrace rice cultivation as well as dry field cultivation. Each household also kept a garden. We were to learn later that until as recently as 1979, two distinct family lineage-specific *shamu jianzhong* production systems had been practiced in Lijiayang, and a separate third system in Linfengkeng. The few questions we had time to ask indicated that these systems had been in practice for at least 150 years and perhaps as long as seven or even eight centuries, depending on which family was represented by the answer.

This multiplicity of people and systems made Lijiayang and Linfengkeng a gold mine for the type of information I was seeking. Not only would it be possible to study the ecological knowledge underlying the *shamu jianzhong*, but in three distinct cultural variants. Plus, I had family just down the road, the surest guarantee possible that I would be permitted to return and reside with the villagers as they went about their lives. The ride back to Kengdi in what had degenerated into a hard, freezing rain neither dampened nor chilled my spirits. Ye Nan was also pleased, but with the clear success of his salesmanship rather than what had been discovered.

The young teacher, lacking Ye Nan's commercial skill, met with no success in Anhui. He saw the wisdom of Ye Nan's rule, "You do not speak no any Chinese," but was neither able nor disposed to offer alternatives to the officials' suggestions. He would only translate and ask, "Do you agree?" Later I was to learn that Professor Jiang had telephoned the Forest Ministry office in Anhui advising that "the foreigner" should not be permitted to travel outside of the city. Within hours I was back on the train for Nanjing, relieved not only to have found a suitable study site, but also without any justifiable reason to cause either Dr. Hsiung or Professor Jiang to lose face.

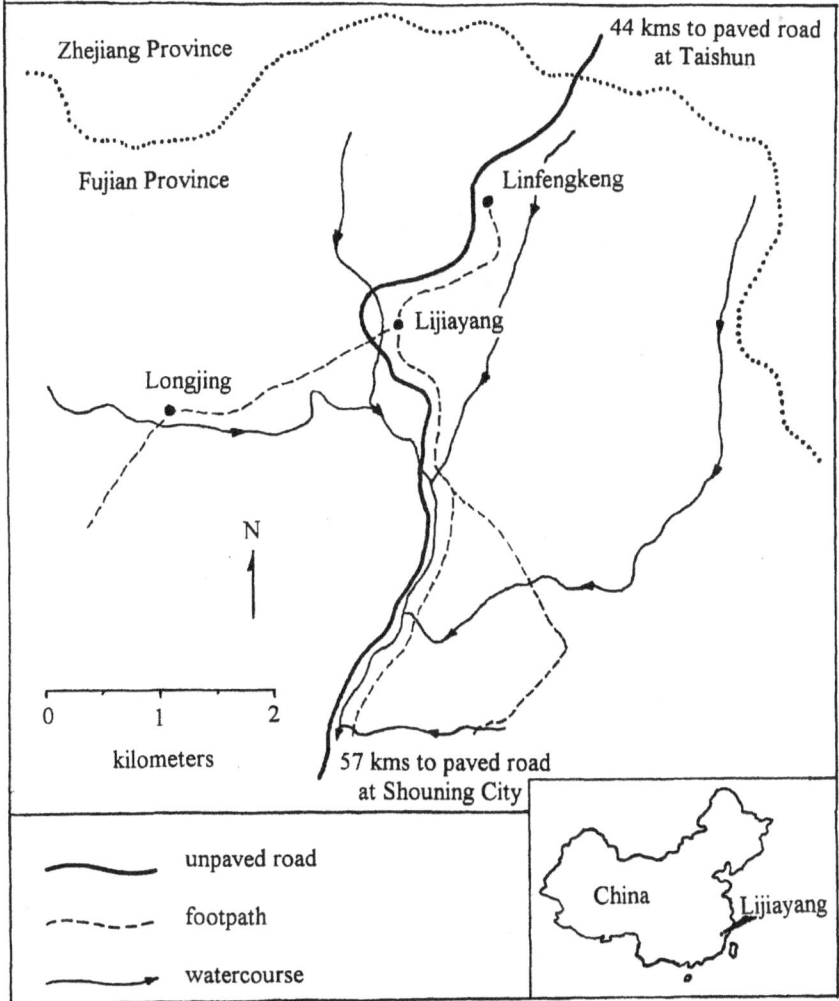

Map 3.1. Lijiayang, its neighboring villages in Shouning County, and their approximate location within China (inset).

NOTES

1. Paul Chandler, *Ecological Knowledge in a Traditional Agroforest Management System Among Peasants in China* (Ph.D. dissertation, College of Forest Resources, Univ. of Washington, 1990), 78–87.

2. Yu Xintuo, *Shanmu* (sic), (Fuzhou: Fujian Science and Technology Press, 1983) (Chinese).

3. ———, pers. comm. (President, retired, Fujian Forestry University, January 19, 1988).

4. Edgar Snow, *Red Star over China*. (New York: Modern Library, 1938), 189–208.

5. Chen Changfa, pers. comm. (Lijiayang Village Party Secretary, Lijiayang, Fujian, January 25, 1988).

6. Lie Demiao, pers. comm. (Secretary, Linfengkeng Village Committee, Linfengkeng, Fujian, January 25, 1988).

7. David Jeffrey, Frances W. Schaffer, and Polly McRee Brown, "The People's of China," map insert in *The National Geographic,* (Washington: National Geographic Society, October, 1982).

Chapter Four

Sustainability as Once Practiced

During the late 1950s, China's policy of "take space for time" employed widespread and time-tested indigenous knowledge of various forms of the *shamu jianzhong* held by the peasantry of South China in a widespread collective effort at increased agroforest production. This policy caused the *shamu jianzhong* system to be employed on a scale of hundreds, sometimes thousands of hectares at a time. While the practices were ecologically sound on the smaller traditional household scale of one or two hectares, on this collectivized scale they resulted in "great losses" from uncontrolled water runoff and soil erosion in the mountains and down-slope damage to terraced fields, canals, and reservoirs.[1] These "Great Leap Forward" problems were soon compounded by the deforestation for charcoal production in the infamous "backyard steel furnaces" of the "take steel as the key link" period in Mao's ever evolving oxymoronic theories of permanent revolution and industrial development.[2]

Rather than acknowledge a failure of collectivism or central planning, the state labeled the traditional practices of the *shamu jianzhong* "backward" and a major cause of rural China's agricultural and silvicultural problems.[3] After the 1960–61 famine, common traditional system features like broadcast burning, agricultural intercropping, and regeneration from root-collar sprout cuttings, coppice, and wild seedlings (wildlings) were expressly forbidden by law. Only spading was permitted for site preparation and only transplanted seedlings from state forest farm nurseries were considered a legal "production forest."[4] The elimination of the *shamu jianzhong* also meant the elimination of the associated sources of food for the highland village cultivators as well as their incentives to restock, tend and protect some of the most valuable forests in south China.[5] And last as well as least, for me it eliminated any

31

opportunity to study the system and acquire the greater detail of indigenous knowledge afforded while still in practice.

This last detail meant that any study of the knowledge underlying the traditional *shamu jianzhong* would necessarily be purely cognitive; that is, it could only tap into the minds of these villagers and not be aided by any of the observation of participant observation. Fortunately, the professors of my graduate committee had provided me with the theory, methods, and skills needed to at least give it a shot.

DEVELOPING, AND EXECUTING, A METHODOLOGY

As an exercise in ethnoecology, the study of culture-specific systems of resource management, the great temptation was to engage in a merely descriptive study rather than one that generates and tests a falsifiable hypothesis.[6] The hypothesis generated to guide the research held that local villagers would be able to provide descriptions of the ecological processes at work within the *shamu jianzhong* that were functionally equivalent to those derived through application of the scientific method.[7] Clearly, the differences in education between rural villagers and scientists, and hence the terms each would use to express knowledge, meant that any methodology needed to test this hypothesis would be necessarily complex and would require a reasonable mastery of Mandarin as well as local dialects of Chinese.

One of my more anal colleagues never failed to "correct" the use of the word "methodology." He insisted it was strictly "the study of methods." We will go a bit further in Webster's and apply the "set of procedures" aspect of the term.

Those procedures were fairly straightforward, but extraordinarily consuming of time, paper, and patience. First was to verify the salience of the *shamu jianzhong* in the villagers' cognitive domain.[8] In other words, make sure it stands out in their thoughts or memory. Second, a step-by-step decision tree of the local management system would have to be built to a level of detail where each point of decision had only two possibilities.[9] This involved a series of questions, basically "What do you do then?" or "What would you do if this were not possible?" and "What is necessary for it to be done this way?" and so on. Somewhere between four and six villagers would be sufficient at this point. The answers would then all need to be tested for accuracy with two or three different villagers.[10] Third, each two-possibility decision node in the tree that had even a remotely ecological basis would be identified and the reasons for the decisions taken determined. To maximize the number of villager accounts of ecological knowledge, this third step involved the first and second sets of villagers in a similar series of questions flowing from the "What is necessary?" and "What is best?" variety. And, of course, these answers would need to be tested for accuracy with yet a third set of two or three villagers.[11] Last, and finally back in Nanjing, descriptions in the scientific literature of the knowledge regarding the same decisions would be located and reviewed for functional equivalence. While "the literature" was all but certain to contain mechanistic descriptions, the expectation was that villagers' descriptions would take the form of teleologies, anthropomorphisms, morality tales, and the like.[12]

The differences in the forms of description within each account of ecological process illustrate the "emic-etic" distinction central to the ethnoscientific approach to ethnography. An "emic" description is one presented in the local culture's own terms.[13] It utilizes the locally recognized features, the locally employed contrasts between features, and the local terminology to identify, as French wrote, "not only the structural units but also the classes to which they belong."[14] Sturtevant described the utility of this approach: "An emic analysis should ultimately indicate which etic characters are locally significant [and useful for a] reduction of the significant attributes of the local classifications in culture-free terms."[15] These culture-free, or etic, terms are actually the terms or units employed in modern scientific investigation.[16] For example, the emic folk taxonomies elicited by an ethnobotanist would be compared to and contrasted against the etic taxonomies derived through systematic botany. Such systematically derived points and frames of reference serve as what Hunn called an "etic grid" upon which the emic description may be plotted.[17] It is this feature of the ethno-scientific approach, specification of the relevant scientific terms and units that provides opportunities for replication, which is the strength of this approach to ethnography. In this case, the functional process contained within each villager's emic account would be the unit of analysis.

The first step of data collection was most encouraging. When asked individually, fifteen of thirty male villagers answered "*shamu*" first in lists of varying length when asked, "What's on the mountain?" Thirteen said "forest". When they were asked, "What's in the forest?" each began a list with "*shamu*".

The remaining two said there was "nothing on the mountain." They continued to insist, even when their eyes were directed to the forests on the surrounding mountains and they were asked "What types of trees are up there?"

"*Meiyou*." Nothing.

Despite this surreal mystery, I was overjoyed to discover the wisdom of Dr. Hsiung's recommendation. That meant no excruciating conversations once back in Nanjing. According to the formula I had worked out, and even before plugging the thirty villagers' responses into that formula, to these villagers *shamu* was plainly the most salient thing within the mountain forests of Lijiayang and Linfengkeng. That formula calculated the salience of any item on the respondents' list to be the product of the frequency of that item on all the lists, 28 out of 30 in the case of *shamu*, times the result of the mean rank order of the item on the lists on which it appeared, one-point-zero in the case of *shamu*, subtracted from the total number of different items mentioned in the respondents' lists.

The singular prominence *shamu* held in the minds of at least 28 out of 30 these men documented the salience, and hence the potential for useful data.[18] Learning of this encouraging result, Ye Nan was duly proud of his triumph in a difficult job of salesmanship. As for the two that failed to support the salience of *shamu* as a productive domain of inquiry, Ye Nan wrote them off as fools. My own feeling was that we were missing something.

The second step proved much more complex. It was soon realized that three separate management systems had been practiced as recently as ten to twelve years earlier, two in Lijiayang and one in Linfengkeng, and each unique to the two villages' three main *xings*. While a data bonanza, this meant three separate decision tree models would have to elicited[19] and wrestled with separately through all remaining steps of the procedure. It also meant that locating a sufficient number of separate informants for the model-building and model-testing phases from the two smaller *xings* would be especially difficult,[20] probably impossible if reluctance to spend time talking with outsiders arose for whatever reason. And of course, the six-month permit cheerily provided by my cousin Zeng meant Ye Nan and I were going to try the patience of everyone, especially those we lived most closely among in Lijiayang.

While Ye Nan's ability to "sell ice to Eskimos" is probably legend throughout Ontario's insurance industry today, his inability to live among rural villagers no doubt lives on in Lijiayang. This misfortune was only partly of his own making.

In addition to Ye Nan, the *xing* Ye, or "leaf," applied to thirteen households in Lijiayang. While this facilitated our interactions with those households, the other 78 households often had a question or two that reminded us, despite my well-placed "family" in Kengdi, a "business card problem" could happen here as well. While a repetition of that miscommunication never arose in Ye Nan's case, his familiarity with the children of Wu Zaiyuan, our host, did breed contempt.

The two oldest of Father Wu's three pre-one-child policy children disliked Ye Nan for similar reasons. The son, the older of the two and the one person who did the most and the heaviest of the family's labor, soon grew annoyed at Ye Nan's frequent philosophical disquisitions on China's bright and sure potential for the future recovery of its past glory. Ye Nan, a soft and pampered momma's boy as well as dreamer and idling intellectualizer, was all and exactly what the eldest son was not. The farmer's daughter agreed and found Ye Nan's confidence that "all the young girls want me" as absurdly laughable as the young women studying back in Nanjing. However, instead of shouting at him as the son had done, the daughter worked on his vanity.

During my four months in Lijiayang I was usually addressed as *"Lao Zeng,"* meaning old or venerable Zeng. And since the tone used to pronounce the name Ye can be changed to render the sound's meaning to something like "again" or "yet more," one can say "older" using the combination *ye lao*. The daughter took this tonal pun, added two more characters, and created the locally quite popular and oft repeated *"ye lao, yan tou,"* yet another of China's many thousands of four-character allegorical morality plays. This particular one was about how as Ye Nan grew older his head, his *touze*, would become rounder as it suffered the retreat of still more hair from an already very high forehead. Within three weeks the daughter had him. He became sufficiently convinced of his impending baldness that he abandoned his promise to assist in data collection and walked over the pass into Zhejiang province to Taishun, pausing there long enough to take the "Miracle 101" treatment for male pattern baldness, as he headed back to Nanjing and home cooking.

By the time Ye Nan cut out, we were a fair way into the construction of the Ye clan's decision tree, but had little more than a basic outline for that of the Wu, with 74 households larger than the other two major lineages in the two villages put together. And we had even less from the Lei, the Shezu minority clan up the road in Linfengkeng. Not only was the second step of the research barely started, but by being without someone from the university in Nanjing with me, I was also in violation of my cousin Zeng's "closed county" permit as I proceeded on alone.

Ye Nan's aloofness from our hosts had been moderated during our first two weeks back in Lijiayang six months after our initial inspection. We had been accompanied by one of his father's doctoral students, a young, smiling, very happily married man named Sun Duo. He was there to collect soil samples, carry them back to Nanjing, and once there begin a basic soil analysis for structure, nutrients, relative components, pH, and so on. He also helped us collect plant specimens from the transects across each of the "best," "average," and "barely good enough" *shamu* growing sites pointed out to us by villagers from each of the three lineages. Sun Duo got along well with everyone and having been exiled to Tibet as a member of a mixed Han-Manchu family with a "bad class background," he had seen far worse than either Lijiayang or Linfengkeng. During those two weeks he was also the inspiration for the idea that finally succeeded in getting enough villagers to sit for enough time to

slog through the repetitive, boring process of a cognitive ethnographic interview. That idea was to take up smoking. We could buy and share cigarettes
with poor, bored villagers for as long as it took, and they could sit and smoke
for as long as we had cigarettes, and as long as we both smoked with them.

When Ye Nan finally got home, his father exploded, or so I was told as
Sun Duo offered me a cigarette when he arrived, smiling as usual, back in
Lijiayang a few weeks later. With his help, the pace of work greatly acceler-
ated and with almost two full months left on my permit, all the data I could
think of was finally secured. The soil samples, the plant specimens, the names
and genealogies, the sketch maps and decision trees, the interview notes, the
field notes, all of it.

THE WU TRADITION OF SUSTAINABILITY

In 1988 intensive annual agriculture occupied all but two of the 91 households in Lijiayang.[21] These farmers engaged in both irrigated terrace rice
cultivation as well as dry field cultivation of corn, soybeans, pulse beans,
and sweet and white potatoes. Each household also kept a garden to supply
itself with two harvests per year of dietary variety in the form of long beans,
pulse beans, a great number of cabbages, a bit more corn, and a small selection of spices and medicinal plants for household use (see Table 2.1).
Until as recently as 1979, two distinct family lineage-specific agroforest intercropping production systems had been practiced in Lijiayang and a third
in Linfengkeng.

The system of the older and larger of the lineages in Lijiayang, the Wu, was
derived from almost 800 years of practice. That experience had followed over
400 more years of practice in the region of Zhejiang Province where the
Longquan Majie timber scaling rules had later been developed.[22]

The Wus' system began with the harvest of one-hectare or smaller patches
of the existing forest, followed by a burn of the logging slash. While scientists had documented the negative results of fire on organic content and the
structure of the forest soil,[23] as Lan had stated, "For the peasants at present
there is no substitute,"[24] or as the villagers phrased it, "*Huo bu shang shan,
bu neng cha sha*" (Fire not on mountain, cannot insert *shamu*),[25] a phrasing
also encountered by Sheng.[26] Well aware of the potential for fire-caused soil
damage, the Wu waited for a cool, dewy morning to minimize that damage.

Another advantage of a cool fire was its ability to maximize acid neutral-
izing nutrient-rich wood ash.[27] The Wu addressed these two benefits by noting that, in addition to being *hao fei* (good manure), the wood ash kept the
soil from being *tai suan* (too sour).

Once cooled, the site was spaded and then planted to daikon turnip. The root-collar sprouts that emerged during this first cropping year from any harvested *shamu* were cut and transplanted amid a second-year crop of corn, which quickly replaced millet in this phase of the system after being introduced from the Americas.[28] A leafy, high-stemmed crop like corn was ideal to protect the sensitive young *shamu* from soil desiccation and sunscald.[29] The Wu noted the superior growth of *shamu* when interplanted by observing, "When *shamu* is young, corn is its big brother."[30]

Oil-bearing tree crops such as tung-oil (*Aleurites fordii*) and tea-oil (*Camellia* spp.) were sparsely interplanted amid the *shamu* stems at this time as well. If sufficient *shamu* planting stock were not available, the gap would be made up with lifted wildlings of *shamu*'s family relative and community associate *wenmu*, or Chinese sugi (*Cryptomeria fortunei*), but among the Wu, unlike their neighboring *xings*, incorporating *wenmu* was rare and undertaken by them only under necessity. Like *shamu*, *wenmu* had appeared on the lists of the 28 villagers who named trees, but had been second on those lists in all cases. This degree of salience indicated the local importance of *wenmu*, but also its secondary importance to *shamu*.

The Wu preferred root-collar cuttings to other stock for regeneration of *shamu*. Such clonally derived stands suffered less competitive mid-rotation mortality[31] because the "cuttings are all brothers [and] have no jealousy" (*chatiao dou shi gedi de, meiyou hongyanbing*). One villager further noted that *shamu* grew better if it originated from local cuttings than from the seedlings offered by the Kengdi Forest Farm because "everyone is happier closer to home."

Third and fourth year annual crops usually were millet and soybean (later peanut, another New World marvel), respectively. The Wu insisted a nitrogen-fixer like soybean or peanut was critical as a last intercrop because of its ability to compensate for the possibility that earlier intercrops had "taken food from the *shamu*'s bowl." As had Yu and Sun,[32] all but the youngest villagers in both Lijiayang and Linfengkeng claimed such intercropping was beneficial for the *shamu* by making it "more exerting" (*bijiao nuli*).[33] In addition, the application of composts and green and animal manures to the intercrops gave the *shamu* the opportunity "to eat from the same bowl."[34]

By about the 10th year the yield of the oil-bearing trees would decline, but several of the useful invasive as well as planted medicinal plants would be sufficiently mature for annual collecting by this time. By about the 20th year medicinal herb production would be interrupted to harvest the oil-bearing trees and any *wenmu* to gain some mid-rotation income and, more importantly, to thin the remaining *shamu* stand, thus adding high-utility late-rotation wood volume. Medicinal herb production would recover within about five years and continue until the final *shamu* harvest. The Wus' system took advantage of the absence of a board-width feature within the *Longquan Majie* rules, so a roughly 35-year rotation could produce commercially valuable *shamu* and a total of about 20 years of medicinal herb production.

Traditionally, three consecutive rotations were undertaken before the land was abandoned for about 40 to 50 years to a *guamu* (beech-oak-chestnut) secondary forest fallow. *Shamu*-related and other medicinal herbs reappeared in annually collectable quantities by about the 10th year of this fallow and usually remained until the cycle was re-initiated. Unlike *shamu* and *wenmu*, the timber produced during this fallow was of high local utility only as fuel, and its slow growth and poor form made it rarely suitable for more than occasional local furniture production. The many political campaigns rural China suffered between 1949 and 1976 had the result of much *shamu-wenmu* forest abandonment and subsequent *guamu* forest predominance (Table 4.1).[35]

The Wu system has demonstrated sustainability in both its ecological and, as will be demonstrated in the next chapter, economic dimensions by eight centuries of local practice. It matches or exceeds the best economic returns and ecological characteristics of the other lineage-specific system in the village as well as the current state forest farm systems practiced well down slope in central and southern Shouning County. The repeated productive use of the land followed by an extended fallow has maintained local forest community diversity,[38] that in turn has restored forest soil quality and productivity for at least 800 years, a span of time constituting a tangible rather than merely rhetorical indicator of sustainability.

Table 4.1.   Land Areas in Lijiayang Village (hectares)

Annual croplands	21.9
terraced rice fields	17.1
non-irrigated grain and bean fields	3.5
non-irrigated house gardens	1.3
Bamboo groves	45.1
Cultivatable forests	158.2
shamu-wenmu forests	64.3
mixed-age *guamu* forests	93.9
Pine and other forests	383.5
Wastelands, homesites, other	11.4
Total village land area	620.1

Sources: Chen,[36] Shouning County[37]

THE YES' UNSUSTAINABLE LACK OF A
SUSTAINABLE TRADITION

Another likelihood beyond the Wus' system emerging under the 60-year lease terms of the latest "responsibility system" reforms[39] is the resumption of the youngest of the systems, that of the Wus' neighbors, the Ye family lineage. Their *shamu jianzhong* system was derived from much less experience, about 160 years of practice in Lijiayang and about 225 years in another village nearby but at a much lower elevation. Significantly, their move had been prompted by a need to find more productive soils.[40]

The Ye system differed from that of the Wu as *wenmu* were always inter-planted amid the *shamu* in a roughly 3:1 *shamu*-to-*wenmu* ratio. These *wenmu* were thinned from the stand around the 20th year along with the oil-bearing trees. The post-thinning *shamu* stand was allowed to grow, usually for a total of about 65 years before the site was clear felled and the system repeated. The soil disruption of the Yes' intermediate harvest also delayed medicinal herb recovery for about five years. So, in addition to the mid-rotation *wenmu* timber, this system also offered 10-year early and 40-plus-year late periods of medicinal herb production. With no usefully corrective learning experience to the contrary,[41] the Ye believed this pattern could be repeated indefinitely, so their *shamu-wenmu* planting sites were never given over to a broadleaf *guamu* forest fallow.[42]

This no-fallow system was believed by the Ye to maximize economic returns, but by its third rotation it was visibly and severely damaging to the underlying forest soil's agricultural potential. Although their relatively limited experience had given the Ye little or no opportunity to observe its effects, research in China has shown that repeated monocrops of *shamu* tend to lower soil pH, increase concentrations of phenols as well as iron and other metallic salts, and favor the dominance of soil flora adverse to continued *shamu* growth. By the beginning of a fourth rotation, *shamu* growth is greatly reduced and the seeds of the associated intercrops, including inter-planted and under-planted medicinals, often fail to germinate.[43]

The documented adverse soil and plant community impacts of such a no-fallow system were unknown to local officials as well as to the Ye, although several of the Wu farmers speculated on at least some of these possibilities, including adverse soil impacts of this version of the *shamu jianzhong* as the cause of the Ye family's migration to Lijiayang. The Wu further asserted that their version of the *shamu jianzhong* produces both more food and a greater volume and value of *shamu* timber than any other version they have had opportunity to observe, be it that of their neighbors the Ye or their government.

The long experience of the Wu family lineage with their particular form of the *shamu jianzhong* had, in fact, allowed them to understand, recognize and avoid threats to sustainability that scientific chemical and biological analysis of soil properties revealed only in the 1980s.[44] Also significant, the Wus' assessment of the long-term growth of *shamu* from cuttings and the impacts of repeated rotations of *shamu* and *wenmu* on the sustainability of soil quality more closely matched those in China's scientific literature [45] than the views expressed by Bao Yingsen, the Vice-Director of the Province's Forest Ministry, when he briefly visited Father Wu's family to encourage the research to an early conclusion. However, with only two or three years of practice among the younger generation, this indigenous knowledge, despite its validity, had already begun to be lost to the young.

This loss of knowledge combined with the unknowns beyond the locally applicable 60-year lease term means another possibility could be a curtailment of the traditional Wu system after two 35-year rotations; which, likely being repeated by the next lessee, would degrade the forest soil resource at twice the rate of the Yes' traditional system.

This particular example also illustrated the problems a scientist in China may encounter when trying to test the validity of the government's official, ideologically inflexible views on resource management.[46] When asked whether forests were more productive if regenerated from seedlings or cuttings, Vice-Director Bao claimed that the cuttings initially performed better, but those originating from seedlings soon surpassed the cuttings' growth rates. In direct contrast, villagers from both the Ye and Wu lineages explained that just the opposite was true. Their explanation held that while cuttings needed time to develop roots and so grow more slowly in the early years of a rotation, they soon catch up and surpass the growth of trees originating from seedlings. In 1979 and 1984 Lin Jie, a forest researcher working in Fujian Province published a comparative study on cutting and seedling growth rates. His discussion addressed site index and form factor differences,[47] but in an act of political self-defense never so much as mentioned the overall superior growth of the cutting-originated stands.[48] However, he clearly suspected the truth of the villagers' point of view, as the first cut in his multi-block design was the direct comparison of cuttings versus seedlings.[49] While Lin Jie certainly was aware of the significance of this difference, he was also probably aware of the trouble that awaited him were he to contradict, in writing, the official policy holding that "only seedling afforestation can be recognized and accepted as a timber forest."[50]

Despite this grim situation, the Ye provided hope that indigenous knowledge can be rebuilt over time. This hope came in the form of a description of how one Ye villager had determined two to be the ideal number of new stems to leave after a coppice thinning. The process he described was a series of practical tests in which he had left one, two, three, or four stems on vigorously resprouting stumps of *shamu* after a few normal timber harvests. After watching them grow for decades under different conditions, he determined through this observation that, while leaving one stem produced a larger, more useful piece of timber, the greater likelihood of a complete loss of that one stem for whatever reason made that choice undesirable. While leaving three or four stems increased the likelihood of a harvest, the local utility of each piece of timber was lessened by its smaller diameter resulting from the need "to share the food" with the other two or three stems. His process of applied, non-statistical hypothesis testing, or "proto-science,"[51] had led him to the conclusion that two shoots produced the best compromise between security and utility of the harvest. This example of proto-science provided evidence to support a claim by Bloom made in another context of the ability of people "to reason from visible effects to invisible causes and speculate about the intelligible order of nature as a whole."[52]

Still, if this test required decades, and the Ye have not yet produced a sustainable management system by proto-scientific means, one may deduce that the process of achieving such a system requires more than the roughly two centuries they have had to work with in any one locale.

THE LEI TRADITION OF SUSTAINABILITY

In a learning process that requires several centuries, there is no guarantee that two different groups will arrive at their shared goal of sustainability with the same management systems. This fact is illustrated by a comparison of the Wu of Lijiayang with the Lei of Linfengkeng.

As one of the many minority nationalities pushed upslope by the Han expansion into south China centuries ago, the Lei found themselves sitting within easy sight of the crest of the Tonggong Shan dividing Fujian from Zhejiang Provinces. Unlike the two Han lineages in Lijiayang, the Lei were reluctant to share or even discuss documents on family history, genealogy, and land claims. As best as could be determined, the Lei had been in Linfengkeng for at least 250 years, but more likely about 400 or more. Before that they had resided for about 450 to 600 years in an area in eastern Guangdong Province where *shamu jianzhong* cultivation had employed at least three methods of *shamu* regeneration: wildlings, coppice, and root-collar cuttings.[53]

It is possible that the Ye had arrived at their 65-year rotation by following the example of the Lei as, with one significant exception, the system they used was identical to that of the Lei. While the Ye regularly clear-felled their mature stands of *shamu* around the 65th year, at this point the Lei would perform a near-complete, but still only partial harvest, leaving what foresters call "standards," a few of the phenotypically best trees, normally to become the seed source for the next rotation. As the Lei did not use natural seeding to regenerate *shamu* and there was no practical way of moving very large diameter timber to a profitable market, this harvesting pattern of leaving ten to fifteen percent of the mature stems to grow for another thirty years made little silvicultural sense.

The Lei could offer no more justification for their 95-year rotation than to say, "That's our way." Nor could they offer any explanation for why, like the Ye, they do not fell all the *shamu* stems around the 65th year than to say, "That's not our way." Still, cultural and ecological explanations are possible.

One explanation is that the small number of large diameter timbers resulting from their system fulfills a cultural need. While the Lei built their long, two-story *shamu*-wood homes in much the same style as their Han neighbors, their particular version included a base beam on each outside wall that required of anyone entering the home an awkward moment of imbalance as they stepped over the large, solid piece of wood. By requiring such a maneuver, this base beam could possibly function in the same way as doorways that require unwanted intruders to bend over, thus exposing them to easy attack by any defenders inside.

Another possible explanation lies in forest ecology. In addition to providing an early yield of timber, harvesting the *wenmu* from a 3:1 *shamu:wenmu* mixed stand opens the forest floor to sunlight. Such an opening in the forest canopy presents numerous understory plants with an opportunity to use the reduced competition for light and soil water and nutrients to thrive and, for those with the capability, to move into the canopy.[54] A much heavier thinning of all but one of every five to seven remaining stems of *shamu* would present an even greater opportunity for understory components of the stand. And as the eventual canopy dominants in the succeeding *guamu* forest—beeches, oaks, tanoaks, chestnuts, chinquapins, and some of their associates—have evolved to make use of just such opportunities, the thirty-year period when the stand is dominated by the Leis' *shamu* standards offers conditions much like those created by the forest fallow in the Wu management system that repairs the damage done by the three successive rotations of *shamu*.[55]

The Lei provided some support for the ecology argument with their observations that their stands had incurred no reduced growth resulting from repeated rotations of the same species of trees and crops. One Lei villager even speculated much as the literature in China's forest sciences determined,[56] that the Ye will make their soil "sour" (*suan*), or reduce its pH, if they do not allow some *guamu* to grow amid the conifers.

RESOURCE IDEOLOGY *VERSUS* RESOURCE REALITY

Lijiayang was not spared the ills of the Maoist period. In 1958 all but just over 50 of about 275 hectares of the *shamu-wenmu* forests belonging to the village collective were destroyed during the Great Leap Forward and its rural charcoal-burning industrial development campaign to "take steel as the key link." Less than half those hectares succeeded to the usual broadleaf *guamu* forest as the fire-caused soil damage of that exercise in collectivism permitted only a succession of scrub pine forests (Table 4.1). Since that campaign, only 13.3 hectares during the 1976 to 1979 transition period had been opportunistically replanted. In some cases local planting rates have since improved, but local villagers and Shouning County Forestry Bureau officials claimed both afforestation and growth rates have been less than what was hoped. Villagers and district Party officials attributed both to government policies, especially the bans on broadcast burning. These policies effectively eliminated any possibility of *shamu* intercropping or gaining the necessarily associated silvicultural benefits of restocking with better-adapted root-collar cuttings or wildlings or the "eating from the same bowl" benefits of tending, tilling and manuring agricultural, medicinal and oil-bearing intercrops. Without the agricultural intercrops, according to one Wu villager, a *shamu* stand is like a little girl who has lost her mother: "She will continue to grow, probably find a husband, and probably bear children, but she will never be as happy as she could be."

Conversations with local villagers reflected their dislike of not just these policies, but the very idea of the state's claim to all components of property rights in the local forests. These views emerged unexpectedly during interviews associated with the use of fire in the site preparation phase of the traditional *shamu jianzhong*. All villagers interviewed were asked, "If you were busy transplanting or harvesting your rice crop and a fire escaped on the mountain, would you delay any of these practices for two days to fight the fire?" All said "no." Changing the question to a delay of just one day, caused only one villager to change his answer: "No, probably not, but we all should fight the fire." One added, "It's the state's forest. Let it burn."

These interviews also enabled me to make sense of some of the data collected when the two villagers repeatedly insisted that "nothing" was "on the mountain." Returning to these strange answers months later, each of these two explained that, without even the right to take care of the local forests, those forests might as well not exist, or as one said, "Without use, nothing" (*Mei yong, mei you*).[57] In further conversations, these two as well as other villagers more useful in pursuing the research's primary objectives were all in agreement that, without the right to use the local forests and the right to reap the fruits of their labors in those forests, they had no forests and there certainly would be no purpose in tree-planting, intercropping, tending, or perhaps even in combating a local wildfire in what was the state's responsibility.

NOTES

1. Yang Hanxi, "*Shamu* Forest Management Research," in *Thirty Years of China's Forestry Technology and Science*" (Beijing: China Forestry Science Academy of the Scientific Information Institute, 1979) 164–175 (Chinese).

2. Christopher Howe, "The People's Communes," in *China: Yesterday and Today*, eds. Molly Joel Coye, Jon Livingston, and Jean Highland (Toronto: Bantam Books, 1984), 344–346.

3. See note 1 above.

4. Feng Yushen, Li Xide, and Zhu Kaifu, "Discussion of Some Traditional Experiences in *Shamu* Cutting Afforestation," *Anhui Forest Science and Technology* 3 (July 1980): 12 (Chinese).

5. Yu Xintuo, *Shanmu* (sic) (Fuzhou: Fujian Science and Technology press, 1983), 1–5.

6. James P. Spradley, *The Ethnographic Interview* (New York: Holt, Rinehart and Winston, 1979): 30–31, 112–116.

7. Paul Chandler, *Ecological Knowledge in a Traditional Agroforest Management System Among Peasants in China* (Ph.D. dissertation: College of Forest Resources, University of Washington, 1990): 109–113.

8. ——, *Ecological Knowledge*, 93–97.

9. Christina H. Gladwin, "Contributions of Decision-Tree Modeling to a Farming Systems Program," *Human Organization* 42, no. 2 (Summer 1983): 146–157.

10. ——, *Ethnographic Decision Tree Modeling* (Newbury Park, CA: Sage Publications, 1989): 148.

11. See note 10 above.

12. Chandler, *Ecological Knowledge*, 111–113.

13. Kenneth L. Pike, "Emic and Etic Standpoints for the Description of Behavior," in *Language in Relation to a Unified Theory for the Structure of Human Behavior, Part I* ed. Kenneth L. Pike (Glendale, CA: Summer Institute for Linguistics, 1954): 8–28.

14. David French, "The Relationship of Anthropology to Studies in Perception and Cognition," in *Psychology: A Study of a Science*, Vol.6, ed. S. Koch (New York: McGraw-Hill, 1963): 398.

15. William C. Sturtevant, "Studies in Ethnoscience," in *Transcultural Studies in Cognition*, eds. A. Kimball Romney and Roy D'andrade, Special publication of *American Anthropologist* 66, no. 3, part 2 (September 1964): 102.

16. See note 13 above.

17. Eugene S. Hunn, "A Measure of the Degree of Correspondence of Folk to Scientific Biological Classification," *American Ethnologist* 2 (May 1975): 309.

18. Susan C. Weller and A. Kimball Romney, *Systematic Data Collection* (Newbury Park: Sage Publications, 1988): 9–20.

19. See note 10 above.

20. Peter Biernacki and Dan Waldorf, "Snowball Sampling: Problems and Techniques of Chain Referral Sampling," *Sociological Methods and Research* 10, no. 2 (November 1981): 141–163.

21. Chen Changfa, pers. comm. (Lijiayang Village Party Secretary, Lijiayang, Fujian, January 25, 1988).

22. Wu Zaiyuan, pers. comm. made while referring to *Wu Family History* (Lijiayang Village Committee member, Lijiayang, Fujian, October 27, 1988).

23. Zhang Dinghua, "Changes in Soil Physical Properties after Burning the Mountain," *Forest Science and Technology* 5 (May 1985): 20–21 (Chinese).

24. Lan Taigang, *Modern Evaluation of Certain Traditional Shamu Cultivation Measures* (master's thesis, Nanjing Forestry University, 1987): 32 (Chinese).

25. Paul Chandler, "Adaptive Ecology of Traditionally Derived Agroforestry in China," *Human Ecology* 22, no. 4 (Winter 1994): 428.

26. Sheng Weitong, "Site Preparation," in *Shamu*, ed. Wu Zhongren (Beijing: Forestry Press, 1984): 391 (Chinese).

27. Huo Yingchang," The Effects of Soil Quality and Tree Growth of Burning, Site Preparation, and Intercropping with *Shamu*," *Guangdong Forest Science and Technology* 4 (October 1975): 7–8 (Chinese).

28. Yu Xintuo and Sun Peiling, "Forest Intercropping," in *Shamu*, ed. Wu Zhongren (Beijing: Forestry Press, 1984), 436–437 (Chinese).

29. Sheng, "Site Preparation," 392.

30. Chandler, *Ecological Knowledge*, 205–210.

31. Feng *et al.*, "Discussion of Some Traditional Experiences," 13.

32. See note 28 above.

33. Chandler, *Ecological Knowledge*, 205.

34. See note 33 above.

35. Chen Changfa, pers. comm. (Lijiayang Village Party Secretary, Lijiayang, Fujian, September 20, 1988).

36. See note 21 above.

37. Shouning County Agricultural Bureau, *Shouning County Agricultural Divisions* (Fuzhou: Fujian Province Ministry of Agriculture, 1987) (Chinese).

38. Zhang Xianwu, Xu Guanghui, Zhou Xuqing, and Zhou Chonglian, "Repeated Plantations of *Cunninghamia lanceolata* and Toxicisis (sic) of Soil," in *Ecological Studies on Artificial Cunninghamia lanceolata Forests* (Beijing: Institute of Forestry and Pedology, Academia Sinica, 1980): 151 (Chinese with English abstract).

39. Klaus Deininger and Songqing Jin, "The Impact of Property Rights on Households' Investments, Risk Coping, and Policy Preferences: Evidence from China," *Economic Development and Cultural Change* 51, no. 4 (July 2003): 851.

40. Ye Yousen, pers. comm. made while referring to *Ye Family History* (Lijiayang Village Committee member, Lijiayang, Fujian, October 9, 1988).

41. Thomas H. McGovern, Gerald Bigelow, Thomas Amorosi, and Daniel Russell, "Northern Islands, Human Error, and Environmental Degradation: A View of Social

and Ecological Change in the Medieval North Atlantic," *Human Ecology* 16, no. 3 (September 1988): 245.

42. Ye, pers. comm., October 11–13, 1988.

43. Paul Chandler, "*Shamu Jianzhong*: A Traditionally Derived Understanding of Agroforest Sustainability in China," *Journal of Sustainable Forestry* 1, no. 4 (Winter 1994): 13–14.

44. Zhou Chonglian, Xu Guanghui, and Zhang Xianwu, "Effects of Plantation Burning on Soil Micro-organisms," in *Ecological Studies on Artificial Cunninghamia Lanceolata Forests* (Beijing: Institute of Forestry and Pedology, Academia Sinica, 1980), 160–165 (Chinese with English abstract).

45. Zhang et al., "Repeated Plantations," 143–151.

46. Robert G. Lee, "Ecologically Effective Social Organization as a Requirement for Sustaining Watershed Ecosystems," in *Watershed Management: Balancing Sustainability and Environmental Change*, ed. Robert J. Naiman (New York: Springer-Verlag, 1992), 76–77.

47. Lin Jie, "Research on Site Index and Form of Seedling Established Stands of *Shamu* in Fujian," *Agricultural Science and Technology* 1 (January 1979): 1–24 (Chinese).

48. Lin Jie, Cheng Pingliu, and Huang Jian'er, "Growth Investigation and Research of High-Yield *Shamu* Forests in Nanping Houxi, Fujian." *Fujian Forestry Institute Study Reports* 1 (April 1984): 9–18 (Chinese).

49. See notes 47 and 48 above.

50. See note 4 above.

51. Chandler, *Ecological Knowledge*, 1–4.

52. Allen Bloom, *The Closing of the American Mind.* (New York: Simon and Schuster, 1987): 270.

53. Lie Demiao, pers. comm., (Secretary, Linfengkeng Village Committee, Linfengkeng: Fujian, October 21, 1988).

54. Zhang Dinghua, Chen Tiancheng and Zhuang Zaiwen, "Investigation of Mixed Forests of *Shamu* and *Wenmu* in Hilly Areas of Southern Fujian." *Forest Science and Technology Journal* 9 (September 1983): 93–94 (Chinese).

55. Xia Zhennong, ed., *Term Ocean* (Shanghai: Shanghai Dictionary Publisher, 1979), 2–3 (Chinese).

56. Paul Chandler, "Food, Fiber, and Fee Simple Ownership in the People's Republic of China," *Journal of Private Enterprise* 19, no. 2 (Spring 2004): 61–85.

57. See note 56 above.

Chapter Five

"Mr. Grasping-at-Straws"

The three distinct lineage-specific versions of indigenously derived knowledge of the ecological processes involved in the *shamu jianzhong* as practiced in Lijiayang and Linfengkeng had proven a productive focus for testing the research hypothesis. However, despite the ability of the local farmers to describe the ecological processes at work in these systems in truly exhaustive detail, hence demonstrating a "salient domain" of their knowledge, their ecological knowledge was secondary in their estimate of the systems' continued practice and success. The two villagers who insisted that what was "on the mountain" or "in the forest" was "nothing" had shared a hint of the primary condition to be satisfied if the systems were in fact to resume, continue and thrive.

This facet of their problem emerged in 1978. Deng Xiaoping emerged from the Great Proletarian Cultural Revolution not just alive, but as China's paramount leader. Immediately he began an era of "socialism with Chinese characteristics," better understood as limited free markets.[1] One change of this era was the "household responsibility system," policies permitting individual rural villagers to sign lease contracts with the government granting them and their families exclusive 20-year use rights to irrigated rice land.[2] While still required to produce a set per hectare minimum of staple food stocks, any surplus beyond that minimum as well as any non-staple food stocks were regarded as the individual villagers' to do with as they pleased.[3] These policies were "hugely successful" in increasing the quantity, quality and variety of foods available to the Chinese people and made further revisions very attractive.[4] It further reflected the wisdom of Deng Xiaoping's response to his hardcore collectivist critics: "We do not care if the cat is black or white, only that it catches mice."

47

One of the local villagers who saw the potential in the 1978 changes came to be called "Mr. Grasping-at-Straws". Officially retired, Mr. Grasping-at-Straws was a frequent visitor to our host's home, especially whenever Sun Duo and I were reviewing, correcting, transcribing, translating, or generally fretting over that or an earlier day's field and interview notes. He rarely spoke, but would smile, nod his head to express amity or wag it in a polite admiration of our seemingly constant business amid other adult men who usually were standing around doing their patient best to wait for their crops to grow.

When we encountered him on the road up to or back from Linfengkeng or on the paths in and around Lijiayang, Mr. Grasping-at-Straws would do nothing but speak. He would stop us to converse at as great a length as we would permit. His invariable topic of conversation concerned 1300 *mu* (85 hectares) of rocky, scrubby brush land situated on a slope to the east. This patch of scrubland was situated between Lijiayang and the neighboring village of Longjing. Despite our repeated insistence to the contrary, he was certain these two "out-country persons," not just city persons, but a Manchu person and a *Meiguo* person, "had power." His relentless, undeterable purpose was to engage our "power" in reversing an injustice of Deng's reforms by recovering those 1300 *mu* for the Wu of Lijiayang. Mr. Grasping-at-Straws explained that ties of *xing* had been employed and the land had been corruptly awarded to Longjing during Deng's reforms. Their neighbors, the Ye were vaguely implicated, but now that their fellow bearer of this *xing* had been replaced by this Manchu person, the *fengshui*-time continuum was ripe and not to be wasted. He was outside the house wall when we arose, outside the window when we worked with paper, and never beyond sight of us or our likely path as we went from interview to interview, soil pit to soil pit, timber stand to timber stand, hell to high water. Father Wu was our official watcher, but Mr. Grasping-at-Straws had better things to worry about than whether or not we might be spies. Recovering the 1300 *mu* was all that mattered, and as "about 80% of communities experienced at least one reallocation of land between 1983 and 1990,"[5] his obsession was well founded.

The importance of this rocky, scrubby hillside to the Wu finally was made undeniable, not by Mr. Grasping-at-Straws, but by a group of pre-teen girls out collecting fuelwood. These girls, about six or seven in number, were on the disputed hillside hacking at scrub oaks and other saplings with their *kandao* sickles one sunny afternoon during my last two weeks in Lijiayang. I was sitting on another hill reviewing my field notes and thoughts, hoping to catch anything needed but overlooked during the three-plus months so far spent in Lijiayang. Suddenly shouts and screams arose from the hillside. The girls, waving their sickles and following their natural leader, "Blue-Leaf" Wu

Lanye, were charging another, larger group of older girls just cresting the ridge of the hill from the Longjing side.

Blue-Leaf Wu, a brash 12-year-old with a nasty scar crossing her face from one side of her forehead, across an eye, and into the opposite cheek, was defending with potentially deadly force what she clearly regarded as a use right exclusive to the Wu *xing*, regardless of what or when any government had decreed to the contrary. In addition to the sticks of fuelwood, this small, armed, ferocious girl and her troop successfully defended the two most basic sticks in the "bundle of rights" to real private property—usufruct, or the right to use, and exclusivity, or the right to prevent others from using. For the remaining two weeks, whatever data on land claims and timber, fuelwood, medicinal plant, and crop values that could be pried loose from the villagers was collected. While the ethnoecology of the *shamu jianzhong* was an informative domain of inquiry, Lijiayang's assertion of practical ethnoeconomics was clearly a domain of much more critical importance to the survival of the village.

A reminder of the significance of rights to real property in China's villages and elsewhere came in 1997 when the government of the People's Republic of China again revised its policies regarding access to rural land. These changes extended use right contracts in both time and space, including the extension of use rights to rural forestlands.[6] In most cases these new lease contracts permitted exclusive use of forestlands for up to 60 years.[7] Upon reading of these reforms, I could not help but recall the desperation of Mr. Grasping-at-Straws, the fury of Blue-Leaf Wu, and the relative irrelevance of my focus on indigenous knowledge in Lijiayang.

CALCULATING WHAT'S BEEN LOST

Using local agricultural and silvicultural yield data[8] along with simple calculations of human carrying capacity,[9] it was possible to estimate exactly what Lijiayang had lost in 1978. The means was a comparison of the agroforest management systems possible within the 60-year contract provisions to one possible were China to relinquish state ownership of all forestland and permit rural villagers, like the Wu, fee simple ownership of any forestland they wished and were able to acquire. This comparison depends upon four elements.

The first element is the history of the time-tested *shamu jianzhong* presented in Chapters 2 and 4, especially the demonstrably sustainable Wu version of this system[10] and the simpler, soil-degrading Ye version that unfortunately more closely conforms to these new 60-year lease provisions. To proceed from this initial element, the reader should carry away three points. First, the longer rotation Wu lineage system with its embedded fallow period can guarantee ecological sustainability of the soil resource by means of its changes in plant community composition over time.[11] Second, without the guarantee of permanence accompanying an exclusive usufruct within the "bundle of rights" of fee simple ownership, the broadleaf fallow necessary after a century of *shamu jianzhong* cultivation is unlikely to occur. Without such permanence, unsustainable variants are much more attractive due to their ability to capture the value of the *shamu* stand by the end of the 60-year land-use contract term.[12] This could be done through a single 60-year rotation like a slightly abbreviated Ye variant or, even more destructively, through two relatively more abbreviated 30-year cycles of the Wu variant. In either case, these rotations would be without the necessary restorative fallow. Third and last, an ecosystem-friendly 150-year rotation cycle such as that traditional to the Wu[13] is impossible under the limited term of a 60-year land-use contract, thus guaranteeing an absence of sustainability in any *shamu* management systems emerging in south China within the constraints of the 1997 reforms. Only the permanence of fee simple ownership offers real possibilities of either ecological or economic sustainability.

The second element in this comparison uses simple calculations of the human carrying capacity possible from leased *versus* fee simple versions of the system. Data to perform the calculations include local crop production estimates from villagers residing in Lijiayang along with local official statistical summaries (Table 5.1). The relevant formulae are

(1) $A = (2500 \text{ kcal/person/day} \times 365 \text{ days/year}) / \{Y \times V \times (1\text{-}W)\}$, and

(2) $P = La \times U \times \{(h/r)/A\}$

Table 5.1. Typical Crops in Lijiayang (n/a = not applicable)

crop	intensive yields[a] (Y) kg/ha	extensive yields[a] (Y) kg/ha	nutritional value[b] (V) kcal/kg	% loss by waste[a] (W)
rice	3000	n/a	3675	10
corn	2750	3500	4285	5
millet	n/a	2250	4150	10
peanut	n/a	2250	4050	20
soybean	2750	2500	4060	5
other beans	2000	2000	3550	10
daikon turnip	n/a	4550	1335	10
sweet potato	6500	n/a	3580	20
white potato	3500	n/a	2850	10
all cabbages	not known	n/a	<100	20

[a]data derived from local village estimates and Shouning County Agricultural Bureau[14]
[b]data calculated according to Morrison,[15] Winton and Winton[16]

where:

A = area needed to support one person (ha/person/yr)
Y = crop yield (kg/ha)
V = nutritional value of crop (kcal/kg)
W = loss by waste (expressed as a decimal)
P = supported population (persons)
La = arable land area for each separate component of the system (ha)
U = percent land used to produce calories (expressed as a decimal)
h = number of crop harvests per rotation
r = total length of rotation (crop plus fallow periods, in years)

The third element is a comparison of the discounted present value of the timber and medicinal herb crops likely to be cultivated under the 60-year use-right lease and fee simple ownership regimes. The relevant formulae here are

(3) $P = A \times \{(1 + i)^n - 1\} / i(1 + i)^n$, and
(4) $P = F / (1 + i)^n$

where:

P = present value of specific forest products
A = annual value of medicinal herbs
F = future value of specific forest products
i = estimated rate of return
n = number of years

Formula (3) is much better known as the discounted annual payment multiplier,[17] which will be applied to the relatively high-value medicinal herbs occurring within each mid-to-late-rotation of the *shamu* crop. This will produce a present value calculated to the initiation of each medicinal herb-yielding phase of a rotation. To this future "present" value the discounted single-payment multiplier formula (4)[18] will be used to bring the value to the actual present, the beginning of the entire rotation. Formula (4) will also be applied to the future value of each rotation's timber harvests.

The fourth and final element of the argument is an account of the Lijiayang villagers' own arguments regarding the role of property rights in their willingness to practice a system they understand and know to be useful and their readiness to protect the resources upon which it depends.

CARRYING CAPACITIES: WU AND YE

Applying the data from Tables 4.1 and 5.1 to formulae (1) and (2) results in an estimate of only 221 of Lijiayang's 357 persons supported by its intensive agriculture; including 185 persons from the irrigated rice crop, 30 persons from the dry field crops, and 6 persons from the well-tended, vitamin-rich, but low-calorie house gardens.

Wastes, surplus crop production, limited grazing, and continually collected forage supported an emergency-and-special-occasions-only food reserve of 789 chickens, 205 swine, 21 cattle, 11 goats, 2 dogs, and about 50 cats, plus a much smaller draft power system comprised of 4 buffalo.[19] As the problem considered here is not currently an emergency or a special occasion, these livestock are not included in the results of these discouraging carrying capacity calculations.

Clearly, since the bans that eliminated the villagers' last rights to use their land for the *shamu jianzhong* have been enforced, Lijiayang has not been able to feed itself from intensive cultivation alone.

A rough check of the accuracy of this calculation was possible after the 1988 harvest had been officially weighed. Trucks from the People's Liberation Army subsequently delivered the first two metric tons of rice the Shouning County office of the Ministry of Agriculture calculated as necessary to make up for Lijiayang's production shortfall in stable foods. Review of Shouning County Agricultural Bureau statistics indicated that the Lijiayang share of the annual shortfall was almost 26 metric tons.[20] My own shortfall estimate of 34 metric tons includes a likely overestimate of the local caloric intake (2500 kcal/person/day) as, without the aid of any illness, my own body mass declined from 87 kg to 55 kg during just 124 continuous days on site.

It is likely that no shortfall make-up would be necessary were the Wu of Lijiayang village permitted to resume practice of their version of the *shamu jianzhong*, a strong likelihood if the incentives of exclusive usufruct and permanence within fee simple ownership were to apply. The number of persons that could be supported by the practice of this system is calculated to be an additional 133, or all but three of the remaining 136 not supported by intensive cultivation alone. Thus far however, this compares only the carrying capacity possible by lifting the relevant bans and resuming practice of the Wus' traditional multi-rotation, multi-generation system of *shamu jianzhong* to that possible without its resumption, or what has usually been the situation since the early 1960s.

By contrast, the coincidence of the length of rotation of the Yes' version of the system with that of the longest forestland lease terms makes this a likely version of the *shamu jianzhong* to continue in practice under the current law. The uncertainty of even a long-term lease, compared to outright ownership, would also tend to ensure the continued adverse fallow-omitting repetition of the Ye system. Beyond those supported by local intensive cultivation, practice of the Ye version of *shamu jianzhong* should result in an additional 95

Table 5.2. Likely *Shamu Jianzhong* Variants under Lease in Lijiayang

Abbreviated Wu System		Abbreviated Ye System	
years	activity	years	activity
0–4	food crop production	0–4	food crop production
1	*shamu* inter-planted	1	*shamu, wenmu* inter-planted
5–10	oil-seed production	5–10	oil-seed production
15–30	medicinal herb production	15–20	medicinal herb production
30	*shamu* harvested	20	harvest *wenmu*
31–60	repeat	25–60	medicinal herb production
Repeat indefinitely with each new		60	harvest *shamu*
lease awarded		Repeat indefinitely with each new	
		lease awarded	

persons supported, or 51 persons still without adequate food supplies in Lijiayang.

The Ye family's repetitive 65-year rotation, featuring the 3:1 initial ratio of *shamu* to *wenmu* stems, would be easily shortened to 60 years and so would represent one of the two most likely management systems to be practiced under the current 60-year lease regime. The other is assumed to be two consecutive 30-year rotations, as in the first half of the Wu system, without any subsequent rotations or prior fallowing omitted (Table 5.2). Such an abbreviated Wu system sacrifices ten years of medicinal plants production as well as the five most productive years of *shamu* timber production when forced into the 60-year lease mold (Tables 5.3, 5.4, and 5.5).

Here the reader should recognize that the current lease situation[24] in south China favors a version of the *shamu jianzhong* that not only is unsustainable,

Table 5.3. Volumes and Values of Timber Harvests per Rotation

Property Rights and Cultivation Regimes	Final Stand Density[a] (#/ha)	Harvested Volume[b] (m³/ha)	Crop Value at Harvest (T/ha)
Wu system under fee simple ownership (rotation = 35 years)			
shamu	1410	504.4	2522.00
Ye system under 60-year lease (rotation = 60 years)			
shamu	1103	568.9	2844.50
wenmu	356	106.8	106.80
Total	1459	675.7	2951.30
Wu system under 60-year lease (rotation = 30 years)			
1st rotation *shamu*	1410	408.4	2042.00
2nd rotation *shamu*	1410	408.4	2042.00
Total	2820	816.8	4084.00

[a]Density data from Ruan and Dou[21], Liu and Tong[22]
[b]Volume data from Lin[23]

Table 5.4. Present Values of Timber Harvests

Property Rights and Cultivation Regimes	Crop Value at Harvest (T/ha)	Year of Harvest	Present Value (T/ha) of Timber Harvests at		
			2%	4%	8%
Fee simple by Wu system of three 35-year rotations plus fallow					
1st rotation *shamu*	2522.00	35	1392.32	777.38	250.64
2nd rotation *shamu*	2522.00	70	768.66	239.74	24.92
3rd rotation *shamu*	2522.00	105	348.11	49.93	1.13
sub-total	n/a	n/a	2509.09	1067.25	276.69
all subsequent harvests	n/a	n/a	119.29	23.36	0.00
total	n/a	n/a	2628.38	1090.61	276.69
60-year lease by Ye system of one 60-year rotations without fallow					
shamu	2844.50	60	866.95	270.40	28.10
wenmu	106.80	20	71.87	48.74	22.91
total	n/a	n/a	938.82	319.14	51.01
60-year lease by Wu system of two 30-year rotations without fallow					
1st rotation *shamu*	2042.00	30	1127.33	629.59	202.93
2nd rotation *shamu*	2042.00	60	622.36	194.11	20.17
total	n/a	n/a	1749.69	823.70	223.10

Table 5.5. Present Values of Medicinal Herb Harvests (n/a = not applicable)

Property Rights and Cultivation Regimes	Initial Year	Years of Duration	Present Value (M/ha)[a] Herb Crops at		
			2%	4%	8%
Wu system under fee simple ownership					
1st herb phase	15	20	12.15	7.55	3.10
2nd herb phase	50	20	6.08	1.91	0.21
3rd herb phase	85	20	3.04	0.48	0.01
4th herb phase	120	30	2.08	0.16	0.00
sub-total	n/a	n/a	23.35	10.10	3.32
all subsequent harvests	n/a	n/a	1.35	0.03	0.00
total	n/a	n/a	24.70	10.03	3.32
Ye system under 60-year lease					
first herb phase	15	5	3.50	2.47	1.26
second herb phase	25	35	15.24	7.00	1.70
total	n/a	n/a	18.74	9.47	2.96
Wu system under 60-year lease					
1st herb phase	15	15	9.55	6.17	2.70
2nd herb phase	45	15	5.27	1.90	0.27
total	n/a	n/a	14.82	8.07	2.97

[a]Annual cash yield is assumed to be 1 M/ha/yr on all forestland

but also incapable of supporting the existing local population even in its earlier, more productive rotations. This number of persons not supported by local food production would be certain to increase when the Ye family system's soil-degrading aspects began to manifest themselves by the fourth rotation.[25] With a freely available alternative in practice among their neighbors, the Yes' version would not be the one always chosen were both the permanence and exclusive use rights of fee simple ownership available to all the local villagers.

THE VALUE OF FOREST PRODUCTS FOR
OWNERS AND LESSEES

Thus far, the discussion has addressed the important, but non-market values of self-sufficiency in food production and the sustainability of forest productivity in comparing the likely results under regimes of a 60-year lease *versus* fee simple ownership. If it is true, as Deng once observed, "to get rich is good," then to achieve that goal the villagers of Lijiayang must move beyond local self-sufficiency and sustainability and enter into some form of market exchange with or investment in the outside world. Lacking other natural resources, infrastructure, and the location to gain by tourism or trade facilitation, many of the villagers of Lijiayang have joined the world's rural-to-urban exodus. Most prefer to stay within the security of the known but largely cashless economy of their village. Still, they might nonetheless be able to enter local and regional markets as suppliers of at least three commodities: *shamu* timber, *wenmu* timber, and medicinal herbs. Telling examples of the local, regional and even international demand for these commodities before, during, and well after the 1988 fieldwork are apparent.

Regarding timber demand: While residing in Lijiayang one of my housemates was arrested, bound and transported to Shouning city by the local police along with a truckload of bucked Masson's pine (*Pinus massoniana*) timber. He was accused of selling the timber in Taishun, the same small town to the north in Zhejiang Province where Ye Nan had taken the "Miracle 101" hair restoration treatment. This incident revealed a Black Market in timber, the surest sign of unmet demand, and limited need for Lijiayang to invest in additional infrastructure to extract or transport timber. Ironically, the stolen timber had a willing buyer in Lijiayang. This was the villager who had pooled his family's resources to build the chair factory. This workshop made only eight chairs in two years due to a lack of legally available wood from the state-owned forests that surrounded the village.[26]

Regarding medicinal herb demand: On the way to the site to begin the field work, Ye Nan and I were hosted at the Fujian Province home village of one of my graduate students. The student's father was the local medical herbalist, his office the focus of constant daily traffic, and his family the dominant commercial institution of the town and surrounding valley. Even the casual guided-tour traveler through rural China has likely observed, if not recognized, many examples of the social prominence and economic centrality of medical herbalists in these areas. The reader who has visited an overseas Chinese pharmacy, food store, video parlor, or other business has likely observed the international demand for such herbal medicinal products as well.

The villagers of Lijiayang and Linfengkeng who had seen the original 256 plant specimens collected from our site quality transects were able to identify most of the same medical uses—reduce fever, relieve headache, promote kidney or bowel function, extract snake venom, close wounds, reduce bleeding —of most of the same fourteen species later identified in the Chinese literature as medicinals for specific ailments. A huge variety of uses for all but two of the remaining 242 species were recognized with similar uniformity, including an additional 31 species identified as having various medicinal uses not mentioned in the Chinese literature available in Nanjing.

Despite such examples, no usable market price data for either timber or medicinal herbs could be found. This dictated that the present value analyses of timber and medicinals be done separately. Fortunately, the relative utility values of *shamu* and *wenmu* were addressed in several interviews, so their timber value may be analyzed as a single production process. The range of relative utility values was from 4:1 to 10:1, so the ratio most frequently given, a 5:1 *shamu*-to-*wenmu* ratio of per cubic meter timber values was assumed. An arbitrary monetary value, 1 T/m^3, was assigned to each cubic meter of *wenmu* timber, meaning each cubic meter of *shamu* was assigned a value of 5 T/m^3.

Other necessary assumptions regarding timber quantity are based upon tree volume growth,[27] per hectare timber yield,[28] and mortality data[29] from a variety of official and academic Chinese sources. These were combined to produce the per-rotation final stand density and timber volume harvest estimates summarized for the local management systems in Table 5.3. These are the cubic timber volumes to which the arbitrary T/m^3 values are applied to compare the present values of the two systems.

Annual per hectare medicinal herb production will be assumed to be equal for all three systems at an assigned arbitrary value of 1 M/ha, and will be available for cash exchange from the respective systems according the schedules summarized in Table 5.2.

As for discount rates, one applicable and classic truism that must be kept in mind is that subsistence villagers are risk averse. Accordingly, the range of discount rates that will be employed here are 2% and 4%, rates that might seem low to the Western reader but would better reflect the levels of risk and return that would be acceptable to the villagers of Lijiayang.[30] The villagers' worst nightmare, a more inflated level of risk, say 8%, will also be included in the analysis.

The present values of the timber and medicinal herbs calculated by this approach are presented in Tables 5.4 and 5.5, respectively. Beginning with Table 5.4, several scenarios appear plausible. In the preferred low-risk, low-return 2% world of the Wu villager, sticking with tradition, including the pre-Maoist one of fee simple ownership, offers the psychic value of staying with the known. Maximizing his family's wealth also presents that villager with the greatest likelihood of testing Deng's claim that "to get rich is good." However, even within a low-risk 60-year lease environment, the Ye will be encouraged to adopt the curtailed, even more destructive 2-rotation modified Wu system. Within a 60-year lease regime and at a rate of return of 4%, any actual psychic value of staying with the known may suffer a deflation as the present cash value of adhering to tradition only slightly exceeds the most ecologically destructive management system, the modified Wu. And the riskier 8% environment would virtually dictate a liquidation of the forest resource by any lessees at the end of their contracts. In such an environment, a fee simple owner's ability to leverage the value of the land itself might be all that could spare the liquidation of the forest resource.

The present value of the medicinal herb harvests presented in Table 5.5 supports largely the same argument, although not so starkly. The longer duration of medicinal crop production of the traditional Ye system under the 60-year lease regime still does not allow it to compete with a fee simple Wu system, but differences become less pronounced under riskier, more inflationary scenarios.

As these simple calculations demonstrate, fee simple ownership offers greater value to the village cultivator from both timber and medicinal crops under all but the most risky inflationary conditions. Under such inflationary conditions—when all long-term investments come into question—the highly destructive use patterns of the 60-year lease systems effectively compete with fee simple ownership, at least until the adverse impacts on the forest soils began to manifest itself with the end of the third rotation. Were both the timber and medicinal values not indications to the contrary, tradition might well encourage the Ye, or any other rural producer, to stick with a destructive management regime until forest soil degradation ultimately forced them to move on.

UNCERTAINTY VERSUS FEE SIMPLE STEWARDSHIP

For China's rural villager uncertainty is a greater reality than the law, especially a law that has changed repeatedly over his lifetime.[31] The uncertainty and changing conditions of land ownership in the case of the 60-year maximum lease term currently in effect would almost surely result in cutting in two the Wu family's sustainable version of the *shamu jianzhong*; that is, the repetition of two consecutive food-and-fiber producing rotations, the subsequent elimination of any soil-restoring fallows, and more rapid soil degradation than had previously existed under even the Ye family's system. This shortened Wu-lineage system would be able to support an additional 190 persons, twice that of the Ye lineage, at least until the pattern of soil degradation expressed itself about halfway through the second 60-year lease.

Despite the villager's current and well-founded uncertainty, after three rotations over the course of a century, it is certainly possible that confidence in the permanence aspects of fee simple ownership would grow. Given that confidence, both short- and long-term self-interests would be served by stewardship of the villager's resource base; in this case, by a resumption of the Wu family's traditional practice of the *shamu jianzhong* and its restorative fallows. Although it will not be true much longer, a practical guide to such stewardship still lies within the oral traditions of indigenous knowledge among the time-tested Wu. If liberated through fee simple ownership, this locally valid knowledge can again be put to work for the rural villages of China, and the answer to the question of "Who will feed China?"[32] should be simple: The rural villagers of China.

Similar and equally valid traditions are known to exist in other poor, isolated highland villages in the "*shamu* growing region" of south China.[33] Such locally adapted knowledge, combined with self-interest and the exclusive right to use, perhaps serving as financial leverage while fallowed, or sell to others who will use this land in perpetuity, would make resumption more than merely possible. The estimates of present value of the various cash crops from the forests also indicate that whatever hope China has of safeguarding these rural resources, retaining and using the wealth of local indigenous ecological knowledge of how best to manage those resources, increasing rural self-sufficiency and standards of living, adding both options and security to the lives of rural villagers, and easing the pressures of rural-to-urban migration on the nation's urban environment most likely is to be found down the road to private property, and from there perhaps to the capitalist road itself. If the traditions of sustained productivity are to serve the people of rural south China, or perhaps even help them get rich, the villager's fee simple ownership of the highland forests may be not just the best, but the only cat for the job.

NOTES

1. Flemming Christiansen and Zhang Junzuo, "Introduction: The Village Revisited," in *Village Inc.: Chinese Rural Society in the 1990s*, eds. Flemming Christiansen and Zhang Junzuo (Honolulu: University of Hawaii Press, 1998).

2. Klaus Deininger and Songqing Jin, "The Impact of Property Rights on Households' Investments, Risk Coping, and Policy Preferences: Evidence from China," *Economic Development and Cultural Change* 51, no. 4 (July 2003): 851, 853–854.

3. C.Y. Cheng, pers. comm. (Professor of Economics, Ball State University, Muncie, IN, April 7, 1998).

4. Deininger and Jin, "The Impact of Property Rights," 865–867.

5. See note 2 above.

6. See note 2 above.

7. Deininger and Jin, "The Impact of Property Rights," 854.

8. Shouning County Agricultural Bureau, *Shouning County Agricultural Divisions* (Fuzhou: Fujian Province Ministry of Agriculture, 1980, 1986, and 1987), (Chinese).

9. Paul Chandler, "Food, Fiber, and Fee Simple Ownership in the People's Republic of China," *Journal of Private Enterprise* 19, No. 2 (Spring 2004): 61–85.

10. ———, "*Shamu Jianzhong*: A Traditionally Derived Understanding of Agroforest Sustainability in China," *Journal of Sustainable Forestry* 1, no. 4 (Winter 1994): 1–24.

11. Zhao Yi, "A Summary of the History of Cultivating and Utilizing Shamu," *Sichuan Forest Science* 2 (April 1980): 85–92 (Chinese).

12. Jean C. Oi, "Two Decades of Rural Reform in China: An Overview and Assessment," *China Quarterly* 159 (September 1999): 616–628.

13. Paul Chandler, *Ecological Knowledge in a Traditional Agroforest Management System Among Peasants in China* (Ph.D. dissertation, College of Forest Resources, Univ. of Washington, 1990), 149–212.

14. See note 8 above.

15. F.B. Morrison, *Feeds and Feeding: A Handbook for the Student and Stockman* (Ithaca, NY: Morrison Publishing Co., 1951).

16. A.L. Winton and K.B. Winton, *The Structure and Composition of Foods, Vol. I: Cereals, Starch, Oil Seeds, Nuts, Oils, Forage Plants* (New York: John Wiley & Sons, Inc., 1932).

17. Allen L. Lundgren, *Tables of Compound-Discount Interest Rate Multipliers for Evaluating Forestry Investments*, USDA Forest Service Research Paper NC-51 (St. Paul, MN: North Central Forest Experiment Station, 1971): 73.

18. ———, *Tables*, 17.

19. Chen Changfa, pers. comm. (Lijiayang Village Party Secretary, Lijiayang, Fujian, September 20, 1988).

20. See note 8 above.

21. Ruan Reiwen and Dou Yongjiang, "Experimental Research of Different Afforestation Densities of *Shamu*," *Forest Science* 4 (October 1981): 370–377 (Chinese).

22. Liu Jingfang and Tong Shuzhen, "Studies on the Stand Density Control Diagram for *Cunninghamia lanceolata*," *Forest Science* 4 (October 1980): 241–251 (Chinese with English abstract).

23. Lin Jie, "Research on Site Index and Form of Seedling Established Stands of *Shamu* in Fujian," *Agricultural Science and Technology* 1 (January 1979): 1–24 (Chinese).

24. Deininger and Jin, "The Impact of Property Rights," 851, 854.

25. Feng Yushen, Li Xide, and Zhu Kaifu, "Discussion of Some Traditional Experiences in *Shamu* Cutting Afforestation," *Anhui Forest Science and Technology* 3 (July 1980): 13–14 (Chinese).

26. Wu Senrong, pers. comm. (Chair factory manager, Lijiayang, Fujian, August 30, 1988).

27. See note 23 above.

28. See note 21 above.

29. See note 22 above.

30. See note 12 above.

31. Roy Prosterman and Tim Hanstad, *Legal Impediments to Effective Rural Land Relations in Eastern Europe and Central Asia: A Comparative Perspective*, Technical Paper no.436, Europe and Central Asia Environmentally and Socially Sustainable Rural Development Series (Washington: World Bank, 1999).

32. Lester Brown, *Who Will Feed China? Wake-Up Call for a Small Planet* (New York: W.W. Norton & Company, 1995).

33. Yu Xintuo, pers. comm. (President, retired, Fujian Forestry University, Nanping, Fujian, January 19, 1988).

Chapter Six

Survival in the Field

Ethnographic fieldwork often entails risks. The risks differ from place to place, person to person, and culture to culture. The nature of the risks may include anything from poor sanitation and inadequate food to communicable diseases and violence. Fieldwork in rural China has its own specific risks associated with isolation and poverty, but greater risks are much more easily found in urban China, despite the fear of the urban Chinese that "perhaps you will see something bad" in the rural areas.

Preparation for and awareness of potential risks is a must. Simple things such as daily multi-vitamins, care in choosing what to eat or drink, and listening to the inner voice when it says "Run away!" are the most basic preparations and, in my experience, usually suffice. From time to time, a questionable meal must be eaten to avoid offense to hosts, but such gastronomic adventures are often part of the job. And from time to time other adventures may arise if one is simply at the wrong place at the wrong time.

For me, the wrong time and wrong place in China was downtown Nanjing. A few days after I returned from Lijiayang, Ye Nan came by my apartment to invite me to accompany him to the *Longmen Wuting*, the "Dragon Gate Dance Hall." The outing got off to a bad start when the young men manning the gate refused us entry because I was a foreigner. Later, while we stood across the street from the dance hall debating our remaining options for entertainment, we noticed a scuffle erupting near the door to the dance hall. Soon one young man jumped backwards through the small doorway in the building's iron vehicle gate as he thrashed with what appeared to be a razor strop at a second young man who jumped out after him. The first man then turned and ran down the street, which was a wise decision in light of the enormous, and bloody, meat cleaver the second one swung at him. As Ye Nan and I watched

61

the two race away into the darkness, the crowd standing before the entrance to the dance hall began laughing, but at something other than the two armed men disappearing into the night. Curiosity drowned out my inner voice and I went back inside the gate. Ye Nan followed.

The crowd stood in a circle laughing at a third man trying, and failing, to stand up. Every time he got his feet under him and his weight above his knees he would fall backwards again, and each time the crowd roared a bit louder. At first, he seemed to be just one more drunk. My thought was to help him up long enough to get steady and on his way, but as I knelt over him his real problem became apparent. A patch of his scalp twice the size of my hand had been hacked away from his skull, which was clearly visible, and was hanging on by no more than an inch or two of flesh. As I tried to lay the piece of flesh back on to his head the crowd laughed some more, and when I shouted for someone to get a vehicle to carry him to a hospital they laughed even harder.

Ye Nan tried to help me, but not with the wounded man. Instead, he tugged on my sleeve, "Leave him! Leave him now! Let him die!"

It was a horrible mystery to me until a fat policeman appeared. He too focused on me and not the wounded man. "Why is the foreigner here?" he asked as he eyed the now silent crowd. "Who brought the foreigner? This must be part of the foreigner's gang. It must be the foreigner's fault."

With that, I dropped the man, gave him a quick prayer, and took off.

Ye Nan later explained the crowd's laughter and the indifference to the man's plight. "They believe he deserves to die."

Deserving or not, the Chinese perspective was very different from that of westerners, especially this one.

THE AMAZING SECRET VILLAGE DIET

To westerners, especially Americans, diets resulting in dramatic weight loss are by definition "amazing." If such a diet has any sort of Chinese origins, legitimate or otherwise, it is also by the same definition a "secret" diet. But of course, there is no amazing secret to weight loss. One must simply apply some combination of exercising more and eating less. In Lijiayang an effective combination was available, but as the previous chapter's carrying capacity calculations demonstrate, emphasis was necessarily placed on eating less, much less.

Two days after receiving our official travel permission, I weighed myself during the last after-breakfast walk from the Forest Ministry's canteen: 87 kilos, roughly 190 pounds. Thirty-six hours later Mother Wu set an evening meal before Ye Nan and I, our first in Lijiayang. The bulk of it consisted of exceptionally bland, unsalted, and questionably clean rice. There were also a few cut long beans and a small bowl of fried and salted greens and onions, all to be shared by eight, rather than the usual six, people.

After an hour or so of conversation, Ye Nan and I retired upstairs to our rooms. Unlike urban China, rural China often has spacious homes, but electricity is seasonal. Lijiayang, like 90,000 other rural villages in China, had electricity from the low-head hydro up the valley only during the wet months, and even then it rarely accommodated more than a single naked low-watt bulb per room. In this part of Fujian the homes consisted of eight-to-twenty-four-room two-story stacks of *shamu* cubicles. In each of the two sleeping cubicles assigned to us was a pine bed frame with cross-slats covered by a heavy cotton hand-sewn, straw-filled mattress. The US Army surplus DDT powder brought from Seattle killed the fleas and lice, and sleep was possible.

The next morning's breakfast was *xifan*, "washed rice", with perhaps a half-teaspoon of shavings from dried pork and three or four peanuts. The mid-day meal was a beanless version of the previous evening's feast. The "three hots and a cot" cost two Yuan a day for each of us.

Once every week or two Mother Wu would prepare a watery, three-egg soup, but the most common exceptions to the diet were bowls of steamed sweet potato meal. The eldest Wu son, the family's heavy labor supply, ate as many of these as the rest of us combined. On the three occasions when I was able to purchase freshly slaughtered pork, this son was allotted almost all the lean meat that could be trimmed from the fatty rind. Eight or ten red pieces of the rind, fat, and a millimeter-thick layer of meat topped the family vegetable bowl for the next day or two, and the elder son got his share of that fried delicacy as well. Ignoring the differences in workload, Ye Nan complained to me of an injustice. Ye Nan missed the all-you-can-eat rice and vegetables on the day of the Autumn Moon festival, having returned to Nanjing by that time. With those few exceptions, the first day's fare was every day's fare.

This diet was so bland that on some days going hungry was preferable to its repetition. While *xifan* necessarily became tolerable, steamed sweet potato meal never earned a single star of dining pleasure from me. The end result was not only the loss of 32 of my 87 kilos of body weight, but my hair, which had been Indian black, had turned the palest silver gray. By the time I returned to Nanjing my skin looked like that of an eighty-year-old and I was unrecognizable in a mirror even to myself.

Splitting the filling in a back molar four weeks into my stay did not help the situation. The thought of spending the next few months with every bite and sip sending a shock through my jaw was more sacrifice for knowledge than I was willing to make. Obviously, there were no dentists in that corner of the county; however, it seemed certain that if I left Lijiayang I would not be allowed to return and all the efforts made to get there would be wasted. That left only two possibilities: Remove the tooth, or fix the filling. It took little to realize the tooth was not ready to leave its socket, so amateur dentistry was all that was left. At least the local "free market", a chicken coop of a store at the upper end of the village, carried an anesthetic, the clear sorghum whiskey called *gaoliang*. When the bottle was about half-empty I was ready. A small stainless steel probe brought along as part of my plant dissecting kit was heated until it glowed a pale orange. Using the small mirror on my compass, I laid the probe on the filling and with a hammer borrowed from Father Wu I gave it a whack. Such pain I would not wish on anyone, especially myself. The probe was reheated, the bottle of *gaoliang* was drained a bit more, and with three more whacks the filling seemed to be back in place well enough to get me through.

A few months of Nanjing's "free markets," my own cooking, and the time to read, write, and not worry about collecting more interview data or plant and soil specimens put a few kilos back on my weary body. While many tasks remained to be done, electric lights made it possible to do much of it while warm under the covers of my strawless bed.

Running water, a flush toilet, and actual sanitary paper were also great improvements over the morning ritual back in Nanjing. That ritual began by going around to the side of the house, climbing the steps cut into a giant *shamu* stump, waddling along two warped planks, dropping my jeans, and squatting over one of the three enormous wooden tubs. The deed done, I selected a few of the less sharp-cornered chips of bamboo, none of which were double-ply nor enhanced with vitamin-E and aloe. As long as the rains held out, I could at least strip to my under shorts and wash in the shallow stream running past one corner of Wu Manor. For the first few weeks this never failed to attract a crowd of children and adults amazed at the novelty of washing any part of the body beyond the face and hands. When asked, rather than imply a difference in cleanliness, I explained my bathing as a lingering aspect of religion in America. Instead of strange, now I was regarded as merely backward.

"RED-EYE DISEASE"

One of the idle pleasures of second languages is pondering absences in vocabulary. English, because of its historic ability to incorporate the words of other languages as both phonetic and phonemic equivalents; that is, the same sound carrying the same meaning, has the world's largest current vocabulary in common usage and a consequently relative lack of similar absences in vocabulary.

One of the rare absences that speaks well of English-speaking culture is the lack of an equivalent to the German notion of *schadenfreude*, malicious joy at the misfortune of others. While Chinese also has no exact linguistic equivalent, it does have a close cultural equivalent. This is *hongyanbing*, or literally "red-eye disease." It is similar to the Germans' *schadenfreude*, but goes further in that it provides a term for the pursuit through actions or words of the destruction of an envied rival, in addition to the subsequent, clearly malicious joy over their misfortune.

My presence at the Forestry University created an epidemic of red-eye disease. In addition to Pinhead Li's efforts to dissuade any and all students to work with me, Sergeant Li of the university's Foreign Office did what little he could to sabotage my plans as well. After returning from our search for a suitable research site over the New Year's break, Ye Nan advised me to get Sergeant Li started immediately on securing the necessary permit to reside in a "closed county" for several months beginning the coming July. After explaining the situation briefly to him, Sergeant Li agreed to arrange the permits, but toward the end of June when I asked Sergeant Li if he had made any progress in getting the permit, I learned that in the intervening months he had done nothing.

"You cannot go without your permit," he advised matter-of-factly.

Ye Nan insisted that we go anyway, so we went. When we arrived back in Fuzhou two days later, we learned that failing to do his job was not enough for Sergeant Li. After we had left Nanjing, he had telephoned the Forest Ministry office in Fuzhou to inform them that not only did the foreigner have no permit to travel or reside in Shouning County, he had no permission from the university to do his research.

Ye Nan was furious. The Forest Ministry wanted to expel us from their compound, but Ye Nan managed to convince them there had been a mistake not of our making. That gave us enough time to walk into the city's telephone exchange, a necessity as long as the Forest Ministry refused to allow us to use their telephones, and get hold of Dr. Hsiung.

Dr. Hsiung was also furious, but unlike Ye Nan, he had the power to make a difference. He assured me he could solve the problem in a few days. "As far as you are concerned," he said, "I am Deng Xiaoping." So we waited.

I was permitted to leave the Ministry compound only between 9:00 am and 3:00 pm, so for twenty days I laid around reading in our room as Ye Nan wandered the streets of Fuzhou. After twenty days of waiting, Dr. Hsiung secured our permit and we were finally off to Lijiayang. A bit more than four months later I was back in Nanjing. At the Foreign Office, Sergeant Li acted as though nothing had happened, thus saving a little face for the moments he had to deal with me.

But Sergeant Li was not suffering from red-eye disease alone. Ye Nan developed a case when his visa to immigrate to Canada came through a few weeks after our failed dance outing. According to Sun Duo, he had spent his last weeks in Nanjing telling his father's and Dr. Hsiung's graduate students that they should not work with me, that I was "stealing" their knowledge, and that, in general, foreigners could not and should not be trusted. Sun Duo had also been asked not to share Ye Nan's plans with me as he thought I might try to interfere with his immigration. Fortunately for me, most students at the Forestry University were no more impressed with Ye Nan than Father Wu's daughter had been in Lijiayang and he was widely ignored.

Also ignored by everyone from Lijiayang all the way down the mountains to Fuzhou were the obstacles all but my cousin Zeng had placed in my path when I tried to go up the mountains. When the time came for Sun Duo and I to leave, we were the justification for the China's favorite social event, a feast. In Kengdi we were escorted into a dingy banquet room and met by Secretary Liu and cousin Zeng, my official hosts. Well over a dozen different platters were brought out one after the after for an hour, and with each one my hosts refilled my glass with *gaoliang*. The banquet continued until I puked and collapsed. At that point I was lifted by my dinner partners and carried into an adjoining room. There cousin Zeng arranged for me to have an injection in one cheek of my buttocks of who-knows-what. That, plus a dab beneath my nose of an aromatic called *baihua*, "white flower," and Secretary Liu holding me in his arms as he repeated, "*Hao pengyou, hao pengyou,*" (good friend, good friend) eventually brought me around enough to be loaded back into the police jeep that had carried Sun Duo and I from Lijiayang. An hour or so later we were in Shouning city and the farewell feast was repeated, but with more dining options. After my second drunken collapse, I was restored enough to be carried upstairs and put to bed. The next day was spent winding down the mountains to Fuzhou.

Once in Fuzhou a third banquet was arranged for that evening, this time hosted by Bao Yingsen, the same Vice-Director who had appeared earlier in Lijiayang to ask when we would leave. This feast featured dozens of platters. When each arrived the Vice-Director would pick out the choicest morsels, place them on my plate, and encourage me to eat more. Twenty or so platters into this feast came a rubbery, translucent white meat with a ghastly taste and worse consistency in the mouth. I asked the Vice-Director what this delicacy might be.

"*Lingli,*" he answered. "It is very expensive. You should eat more."

Lingli was a mystery to me, but a flip through my small dictionary revealed it to be a pangolin, an endangered toothless mammal with armor-like scales.

Once informed, I asked the Vice-Director if it was not true that the Forest Ministry was charged with protecting China's endangered species.

"Yes," he said. "We criticize ourselves as we eat it."

Maybe wondering if someone would "perhaps make a problem," he chose that moment to stand up and make a one-minute speech about how my ability to endure four months of the hardships of an isolated mountain village should serve as "a model for the cadres" to emulate. Total gloom darkened the faces of the two-dozen cadres. They had been warned. If any of them saw the stewed *lingli* as an opportunity to contract a case of red-eye disease directed at him, they knew where unpleasant tasks might await them.

TIANANMEN AND OTHER FLIGHTS OF FANCY

One of the seeming universals of universities worldwide is political activism. Another seems to be that both university students and faculty constitute a clearly privileged class, especially in China, where only about one percent of any given age cohort went on to any form of post-secondary education. Regardless of country, it seems that what this privileged class most enjoys expressing through its activism is moral outrage over events and matters of which it is only selectively informed and which require a broad span of ignorance. Despite the political control exercised within all its recognized institutions, China was no exception.

Within days after Sun Duo and I returned to the Forestry University in Nanjing, the front end of one example dominated *People's Daily* and its English abstract, *China Daily*. The originating event occurred during a Christmas dance at River-Sea University, another of the many big schools in town. Despite official atheism, broad political control, broader religious indifference, and its very foreign origins, Christmas is one of the most popular reasons for dances, feasts and other parties in urban China, especially at universities.

While the students welcome the foreign holiday, foreigners themselves are not so gladly tolerated. The male Chinese students at River-Sea were particularly disturbed by their many African classmates' success in social engagements with the female Chinese students. This difference was the product of the African students' easy, self-confident interactions with the females and especially their greater financial resources, many being the sons of well-placed diplomatic officials. The intolerance was a blatant racism that manifested itself in a variety of ways. Africans were sometimes spit upon while on buses or even the sidewalks, asked if the color of their skin would wash off, and often compared to apes in conversation.

In Nanjing, the racism of the would-be educated Chinese students erupted violently during the New Year's break of 1989. Following their Christmas dance, male Chinese students at River-Sea assaulted their many dozens of African classmates. Two days after this altercation, the administration at River-Sea decided to reduce the opportunities for these African students to "perhaps make a problem" by enclosing their dormitory within a high brick wall, but the Africans pushed over the wall while its mortar was still wet. After again being beaten by their Chinese classmates as well as university security, they fled to the nearby railway station and barricaded themselves into a waiting room, thus officially making a problem. Accordingly, the People's Police were called in, dragged the Africans off to their station, beat them some more, and with their electro-stun batons vented the usual malice of the sexually jealous toward the genitals of their competitors.

Just like their colleagues at River-Sea, the student activists at the Forestry University and every other university in Nanjing were outraged. Despite the winter cold, they gathered daily at Gulou Square in great, noisy numbers. *People's Daily, China Daily*, and the regional Asian edition of *TIME* were all sufficiently impressed to take and print their photos, and the students were sufficiently savvy to make sure all their protest signs were in English. One giant banner held aloft read "No Offend Chinese Woman." Its immense size dominated the crowd, which, upon close inspection of several printed photos, included only men, just like the group that had filed out from the Forestry University bound for Gulou.

A few days after the photos appeared in the local paper, their absurdity drove the local moral outrage back out of sight, at least for a while. But later that spring the activists got lucky. In mid April Hu Yaobang, Deng's chosen architect and implementer of China's "One-Child" policy, died.

The One-Child policy was seen by China's privileged urban elites as the paragon of China's progressive rationalism. In the crowded cities, space for a larger family was hard to find, and with economic reform taking hold, harder to afford, so a one-child family was an easy choice in urban China. To the university educated, it made sense for the government to pay the expenses of one child, to pay nothing for the second, and to require reimbursement for the first child's publicly funded health and education expenses upon the birth of the third. Detaining a woman, binding her, transporting her in a bamboo cage, and aborting her child were just some of the unpleasant details the educated classes selected to ignore.

The One-Child policy's impact on poor, isolated, and especially uneducated rural villagers was even easier to ignore. After all, as the students often observed as a reason why my research among China's rural villagers was "not very important" was the obvious fact that "these people have no education." To these urbanites, the first question asked of me at every single rural village visited—"In your America, how many children can you have"—was just a detail. Details such as the rural village's need for human labor power in the absence of mechanization; the ancestor worshipping villager's need for his *xing* to live on; the abuse, ostracism, abandonment, and violence directed at women who fail not only to produce a male heir, but burden the family with one more daughter; and the murders of newborn rural daughters are all easy to ignore when scholars and the local press report little beyond the fact that "these people have no education." From this perspective, Hu's passing marked an opportunity for activists to march again, this time to voice their demand that China increase the pace of progress personified by the late Party Secretary. And at the Forestry University, the same students who had organized and promoted the local anti-African rallies in the winter began to lead their classmates to Gulou Square once again in the spring.

While the local holiday outrages had failed to bring about the Nanjing activists' new millennium, this one would benefit from both its national scope and the warm spring weather. What the River-Sea Africans had done to fill Nanjing's Gulou Square, the death of Hu Yaobang had done to fill Beijing's Tiananmen Square, and then some.

For the next several weeks China's "democracy movement" became the primary focus of the world's news. On the shortwave, BBC's World Service spoke of little other than brave students defying China's aging authorities and the Voice of America was nothing less than enraptured with the students' papier-mâché "Goddess of Democracy." Beijing was caught in a growing more-press-brings-more-students-brings-more-press positive feedback loop.

My own thought was that the students would keep at it until May 11, a traditional day for student demonstrations in China. But May 11 came and went and the students stayed in Tiananmen. As former Soviet General Secretary Gorbachev was due in Beijing on the 16th, the opportunity to cost the government face during his visit was too much for the students to pass up. So, my revised end-date of these demonstrations became May 20, the day after Gorbachev's departure. But like the 11th, the 20th came and went and the students stayed. So the government declared martial law.

It seemed a good time to ride my lead-heavy Phoenix bicycle into town to get the first air ticket out of China I could arrange, a flight to Hong Kong a full week later. The university was plainly relieved to see an approaching end to my presence. For the first time in 22 months, the university's Foreign Office attended to a request with agreeable efficiency.

My last hurdle was permission to take bibliographic materials with me back to the United States. Rather than stick out his neck, Sergeant Li pawned the job off on to Dr. Hsiung. All the materials were taken to Dr. Hsiung's office for inspection. The next day he told me all the written materials were no problem, but that "I cannot tell you that you can have the maps, so take them back to your flat." So, while all the written materials were crated up with my personal belongings, all the maps went into a large envelope taped to my back. At the airport the PLA soldiers guarding the airplane did not pat me down.

I was overjoyed to be leaving China.

My joy was multiplied later at my in-laws' home in Manila when the television broadcast what I was missing back in China, the "Tiananmen Massacre." In another ten days or so I was back in the United States and discovered that American journalists had recast the students of the "Democracy Movement" as Tom Paine with a Chinese face.

None of the newspapers or magazines covering the story had so much as mentioned how or how rapidly the leaders of this movement had managed not only to exit China, but also to be enrolled in such universities as Harvard, Yale and Brandeis. Most had gotten to the United States before me, although I had left China well before the People's Liberation Army had gone into Tiananmen. American journalists made no mention that the student "leaders" from Nanjing who had gone to Tiananmen were the same ones their Asian stringers had covered during the anti-African demonstrations in Gulou Square a few months earlier. These journalists also failed to note the distinctly undemocratic irony of these students labeling themselves as "Supreme Commander of the Democracy Movement," "Deputy Supreme Commander of the Democracy Movement," and so on. At least one or two did cover how Wu'er Kaixi, the most publicized "Supreme Commander," had taken over the entire movement with a copy machine, but most skipped that detail, if they were aware of it all. None pointed out that the troops of the largely peasant army Deng had brought into Beijing from China's northeastern provinces were eager to clean out the privileged students from Tiananmen Square. And none noted that by the time the tanks rolled in, these students, who did not frighten the leadership of the country, were greatly outnumbered by urban workers, which greatly frightened the leadership. The elitism of the students did not mesh with what American journalists wanted to be the truth, so they ignored it and continued to romanticize them instead.

Elitist romanticism worked to my benefit once I was back in the United States. For the next three or four years, whenever the research was presented at conferences or submitted for publication it was greeted enthusiastically. No submission of this research for publication was ever rejected. Venues at conferences where the work was presented never failed to be standing room only. The notion that the "simple" villagers of rural China knew as much or more about their local ecosystem and how it worked as scholars and scientists was found by these university students and academics to be fully in keeping with their neo-racist idylls of "people of color," a term that had come into vogue during my two-year sojourn in China. If admiration had been my goal, my research was the open path to achieve it. However, these same academics had less than no interest in arguments favoring private property rights over state management and control of natural resources. These arguments conflicted with their "watermelon" politics; that is, green on the outside, red on the inside. Those deep into green, statist, elitist, and generally collectivist politics were immune to the change that overtaken my own sense of political justice. While romanticizing rural villagers fit their worldview, the idea that uneducated rural people could well manage their own lives, not to mention their local environment and resources, was not. And as I discovered a decade later in Brazil, even less acceptable to western academia's "PC" mindset was the finding that even a small fraction of rural villagers could be anything other than noble, honest, oppressed, and in need of the well honed paternalism of the educated elite.

INTERLUDE:
VILLAGE VISITATIONS

Chapter Seven

Doing Without in the Americas

After nearly two years in China, I had little desire to return. The work there had been successful in that I had learned what I had sought to learn, been able to render it into a doctoral dissertation acceptable to my graduate committee, and turned the experience into a career as an academic. Other than those successes, it was a failure. It had damaged my health, aged me almost beyond recognition, and worst of all, cost me a marriage. Nonetheless, as a tenure-track academic specializing in the ethnoecology of rural villages in the developing world, it was all but certain that the future would find me in places as poor and isolated as Lijiayang. Fortunately, my knowledge of languages other than English did not limit my options to China.

A decade before I had gone to China, I had been a volunteer in the Peace Corps in Brazil before Jimmy Carter's sanctimonious naïveté had motivated the Brazilians to end the program there. That experience, including an ill-considered trip through Argentina at the peak of its "dirty war," had given me a strong command of Portuguese and a so-so one of Spanish. These dictated that opportunities to continue to pursue ethnoecology would lie to the south rather than the east.

Another advantage for ethnographic research in Central and South America is the presence of a great variety of indigenous populations. These are the only populations in these regions to have lengths of time in place comparable to that of either the Wu in Lijiayang or the Lei in Linfengkeng. As the research in China revealed, such time is a necessary condition for people to generate valid and detailed knowledge of the workings of local forest-dominated ecosystems. And while the unmixed indigenous populations amount to only one or two percent of the more than half-billion people of Central and South America, they have a strong romantic appeal to those making the decisions within both the public and private agencies that make ethnographic research funds available to scholars. By comparison, non-indigenous rural villagers account for about half of the people in those regions, giving any research among them a far broader applicability, not to mention an absence of any need for me to invest the months needed to learn another new language. Still, if the external validity of the findings from the China research was to be enhanced, the indigenous populations were the only ones offering that opportunity.

As luck would have it, the opportunity arose in 1993 to travel to Costa Rica, albeit leading a dozen students with nearly as great a romantic interest in "the rainforest" (as if there were only one) as in sun, sex, alcohol, and sandy beaches. To these students, both indigenous communities and rural villagers were, at best, just one more tourist attraction and, at worst, one more chance to show their peers how much they "care" about the disadvantaged.

Another lucky break came in the form of a person at my university who, on his own authority, could provide me with a thousand dollars to search Costa Rica for research opportunities. He was a chronic alcoholic, which meant that if I could park myself in a chair in his office at the right time, his desperation to be rid of me could be rendered into cash. It worked to the tune of $1500, enough to fund three or four weeks of searching.

The sixteen long, trying days of shepherding through Costa Rica the sons and daughters of affluent families finally came to an end, I bid them a much longed for goodbye, and turned my attention to the Talamanca Reserve on the Caribbean border with Panama.

WITHOUT MEN AMONG THE TALAMANCA

The Talamanca of Costa Rica are one more rural population headed for the cities on the installment basis. Their territory occupies the southeastern corner of the country and stretches from the coast to the mid-slopes of the cordillera that bears their name. Their numbers range from two to five thousand, depending on which source is consulted, and they speak either Cabecar or Bribri, related indigenous languages about as dissimilar as Mandarin and Cantonese. Like Chinese, these languages are tonal; that is, mere inflection can make great changes in what one is trying to say. Like English, these languages are also morphological; that is, they possess complex verbs with number and tense. In other words, the languages have the most difficult features of both English and Chinese.

One professor at the University of Costa Rica was paid to teach Cabecar, but seemed to take such great pleasure in being one of the few non-indigenous Costa Ricans who could speak it that he had no detectable desire to change that circumstance. Like those of his social class south of the border who could make the claim, he never missed an opportunity to inform all his new acquaintances, "My family is Castilian." He further refused to descend far enough to inform me of who might serve as a teacher to prepare me to apply the language. His ex-wife, whom by chance I met the day after the fruitless encounter with him, had many perceptively bad things to say about the man. This meant I would have to learn Cabecar and Bribri as I had Spanish in Argentina, on my own, but hopefully not with a gun in my nose this time.

Thus unprepared, I headed for the village of Bribri a few miles inland from the tourist beaches beyond the Rio Estrella. Bribri is the gateway to the Talamanca Reserve, the least developed of Costa Rica's many Indian Reserves. Once again, good fortune smiled on me, this time in the form of Pedro, a Talamancan man who wanted a ride up the rough dirt road to Shiroles on the Rio Telire. There we picked up two Talamancan teenagers who had been detained, and apparently beaten, by the Policia Rural, the biggest and meanest officers of the law the country had to offer. The policemen warned the boys not to be "*paseando*," roaming around. The man who earlier had introduced me to the ex-wife of the Castilian said such realities were the "dirty secret" of Costa Rica.

Once the two boys were collected, Pedro directed me back through Bratsi, where the boys got out of my rent-a-jeep, and on across the Rio Urén. From there we forded the river again to reach Amubri, a small Indian village of a dozen or so homes built of cane and thatch. In the middle of the village a group of Japanese a few months earlier had paid the locals to build a tall, ramshackle wooden tower from which they could survey the surrounding countryside. Pedro had no idea what it was for and I was more interested in the variety of slash-and-burn plots we found from time to time, including the largest one I had ever seen anywhere. Except for the large plot and two or three others, most were obviously long abandoned. That was not a good sign.

From Amubri we returned to Shiroles and followed the Rio Telire up to a place called La Pera. There we found a few small scrubby slash-and-burn plots being worked by four households, none of which had a male above the age of twelve. The men were all living and working off the Reserve in Limón or San Jose. The poor quality of the plots was the result of the absence of the men needed to fell the larger trees in the surrounding rainforest. With no heavy labor power, these households were forced to slash and burn previously worked plots that had recovered from earlier cultivation no more than to contain brushy vegetation of small diameter. This meant that for my research purposes the older indigenous systems were effectively extinct, and the newer ones had yet to benefit from much or any proto-scientific inquiry among the Talamanca. Still, the proto-scientific process of acquiring ecological knowledge could be studied by rendering "how do you" questions into "how would you do" ones, so the trip did not appear a total waste.

A return trip in 1995 revealed that in the interim the efforts of the first trip had evolved to become a waste. It seems that the tower in Amubri had been built as the first stage of a destructive mining operation financed and conducted by a joint Japanese-Costa Rican consortium. Many more of the Talamanca had abandoned their homelands for the cities, including Pedro and the families I had met in La Pera. The town of Bribri had become little more than an off-reserve haven for alcoholics hoping to avoid the local Policia Rural.

WITHOUT RIGHTS AMONG THE KAÏNGÁNG

The next exploration for a possible research site during the 1996–97— semester break was even more depressing. A group composed largely of current and retired American university faculty, Indiana Partners of the Americas, contacted me with a request to travel to Rio Grande do Sul, the southernmost state in Brazil. Their purpose was to determine if there were some means by which the group and its Brazilian counterpart could be of assistance to the Kaïngáng, an indigenous population scattered across several reserves along the Rio Uruguay that separates the state from Argentina. The same man that had funded my earlier search in Costa Rica further tempted me by noting, "You could even do some more of your research down there."

Of the three reserves visited, the Inhacora and Miraguaí Reserves were largely devoid of any Kaïngáng. Most had already migrated to Pôrto Alegre or other cities in the south of Brazil. The non-Indian population was also in the process of migration. Driving from my base in Ijuí, groups of the *posse terra*, the "possess land" squatters of southern Brazil, could be seen taking up residence along the highways of northwestern Rio Grande do Sul. Some had pitched camp in the rights-of-way beside the highway and some in the median strips between the lanes. The near monopoly of land ownership by Brazil's have classes, land consolidation by international agri-business,[1] and Brazil's supposedly pro-environment "green tree" laws that prohibited clearing new lands together had denied these rural have-nots all but the most temporary alternatives to joining the country's rural-to-urban exodus.[2]

The third reserve was home to the tiny Iraí band of the Kaïngáng. The mere fact that they were still in place was the only hopeful sign so far encountered.

Unlike the populations that most concerned me, the Kaïngáng were neither cultivators nor rural villagers. Until confined to the reserves in the second half of the 20th century, the Kaïngáng had been hunter-gatherers. Today, those who have not abandoned their reserves are full-time wards of an ungenerous, unconcerned, and uncomprehending state.

The Iraí were the most miserable people I had ever seen. The few dozen still on their reserve lived in homes built of black plastic bags stretched over branches either fallen or cut from the scrubby trees that dominated the plant communities growing from the thin rocky soil. Most of their misery was directly attributable to the elitism of Brazil's educated classes and their internationally fashionable, democratically renewed infatuation with "the environment" (once again, as if there were only one).

The first assault on the Iraí Reserve came with the end of Brazil's military government and the election campaigns in the early 1990s. To make it more convenient to engage in local election campaigning, the largest piece of level land on the reserve had been taken and covered with a 1500-meter tarmac airfield that, according to the Iraí, had only been used during the run-ups to elections. That robbed them of any opportunity to become cultivators. After the elections, laws to protect Brazil's wildlife robbed them of any chance to return, even as an avocation, to their hunter-gatherer mode of subsistence, and the green tree laws made cutting any native species of tree illegal. These laws, combined with the depth of their poverty, meant that their fragile, dilapidated homes were all they could hope for. As a result they found themselves, along with their dogs, living ten or twenty to a garbage bag.

Upon my return to the United States, I drafted a bi-lingual report for the Partners. It suggested that if they were serious about improving the lives of the Kaïngáng, both the Hoosier and Gaúcho elites should use their personal political contacts to restore to the Iraí and other bands their full rights to the property on which they lived; that is, exempt them from Brazil's anti-human, pro-environment laws and permit them to till, hunt, gather, or even build a casino if they so desired. Like most such elites, despite their obsessive wallowing in pity for the less fortunate, they were uncomfortable with the idea of allowing people less educated than themselves to make their own decisions regarding the course of their lives. Much like my students in China who feared that "if people have too much freedom, then they will have sex," both the American and the Brazilian elites feared that if the Iraí had too much freedom, then they might cut a tree and build themselves a decent home. Indira Gandhi's observation that "poverty is the greatest environmental threat" was lost on them. Instead of protecting their property rights and thus liberating them, the Partners wanted to know "what we can give them." Continued paternalism was clearly their preferred option.

WITHOUT LITERACY AMONG THE MAYA

Returning from Brazil, it was obvious that ethnoecology had played itself out for me. Not only would a new locale for research be needed, but an entirely new field of inquiry would be needed as well. Once again, good fortune appeared, this time in the form of Germán Cutz, a student from my rural development and graduate research classes who was pursuing a doctorate in adult education. Germán was Guatemalan and a Maya. Several months before my trip to Brazil, he had approached me to help design doctoral research to learn why the rural Maya do not participate in the adult literacy programs available to them[3] and, with the literacy they would acquire, improve their economic and political options. He stressed that what interested him was not participation, but rather non-participation.

While I had hoped to travel with him to Guatemala to search for one last shot at ethnoecology, he advised that my presence would tend to close the doors of Mayan households to his inquiry as well as place us, especially him, in danger of potentially deadly run-ins with the local non-Mayan police. We were both glad he did not need me to accompany him.

Dr. Cutz arrived at some convincing findings. It seemed that the Maya confront a series of largely self-imposed deterrents to participation in adult literacy programs. These deterrents exist at four distinct levels.

At the level of the individual, the Maya believe literacy does not address their personal needs and that tasks requiring literacy are not work. There is also the perception among Mayan adults that schooling is suitable only for children.[4]

Within the Mayan family there is a rigidity of family obligations and moral values; that is, women must manage and maintain the household and men must work in the fields and forests to support the family. Also among the men there is a fear of humiliation lurking within a classroom to undermine their sense of *machismo*. There is the additional cultural value that young people disrespect their elders and are trying to be better than them by acquiring literacy.[5]

Within the Mayan community there was great pressure to maintain an uncompromised Mayan ethnic identity, to demonstrate loyalty to the Mayan community, and not to assume outward manifestations of the *"ladino"* such as pressed trousers, store-bought shoes and shirts, and speaking Spanish. As there are no written versions of the several Mayan languages, literacy necessarily means Spanish, so literacy offers no options to the Maya beyond these outward manifestations of cultural abandonment. Also, a Maya is usually able to "borrow literacy;" that is, to have a literate acquaintance intercede when literacy is needed to complete forms or other documents.[6]

At the national level, Guatemala's education budget is heavily weighted toward urban and non-Mayan rural areas of the country. In addition, the approaches to teaching are designed for formal learning styles more suitable for preparing students to assume wage and salary jobs. By contrast, the Mayan teaching style uses observed examples and only during opportunistic moments, such as when a child asks a specific question, is direct explanatory teaching employed.[7]

For me, the idea of non-participation itself was the most interesting discovery. Dr. Cutz's work had reinforced suspicions that had emerged from my reading, my professional experience, and the experience of growing up in the rural south of the United States. Non-participation in assistance programs is more often than not dictated by the design of the programs than any reluctance on the part of rural populations.

PARTICIPATION AND NON-PARTICIPATION

As the World Resources Institute once asserted, "improving the quality of life in rural communities is a primary goal of development."[8] My concern was with those households that seem to defy the assumption that "rural people can be agents of their own development."[9] Increased socio-economic differentiation, often if inexactly expressed as the rich getting richer and the poor poorer, has been a frequent unintended consequence of efforts toward social and economic development. Accordingly, it should come as no surprise that non-participants in rural development assistance often include the poorest of the poor, be their poverty relative within their own social class[10] or merely their sex.[11] This non-participating segment of rural society is also largely omitted from the current literature on participation and participatory methods in rural development, despite expressed intentions to "put the last first."[12]

Participants, by definition, participate in the research or practice of rural development, thereby facilitating data collection, project implementation, and diagnostic feedback. Precisely because they do not participate, non-participants are inherently a more difficult population to study,[13] much less approach with changes designed to improve their quality of life. Questions of who are non-participants and what are their qualities of life, much less why non-participants actively or by default choose not to participate, can hardly go beyond philosophical and ideological debate until these people are characterized and the reasons they report for their choices are elicited, verified, and analyzed.

A classic example of non-participation and its resulting unintended differentiation is the Green Revolution of the 1960s and 1970s. This agricultural development technology was designed to bring, along with peace, greatly increased crop yields to the rural households of the developing world.[14] The Green Revolution achieved this goal in the aggregate and among those households able to participate in it. However, participation required the ability to put together capital for genetically improved seed, fertilizers, usually pesticides, often mechanization, and some times precise water management. A sufficient area of tillable land to gain the economies of scale was also needed to balance the relative capital intensity of the technology. Rural households lacking the necessary land and capital to participate in the Green Revolution saw their quality of life decline in relative and often absolute terms, especially if their small landholdings were aggregated into larger parcels or their labor displaced by machines.[15] Rural households not participating in this technology were or became the poorest of the poor, migrated to cities, and had lives offering the qualities of deprivation and insecurity.[16] For these households, non-participation was dictated by landlessness and poverty, which ultimately led to still greater landlessness and poverty. What happens to the rural people displaced by such differentiation remains a troubling question to this day.

Early presumptions by academic experts and development practitioners that they knew best what the poor needed resulted in misguided efforts toward social and economic development assistance for the poorest of the poor. Illustrative of these phenomena is the analysis by Mamdani[17] of the "Khanna Study" of family planning and population control in a rural village in India by the Harvard School of Public Health.[18] Mamdani's analysis revealed that a woman's "acceptance" of contraceptives when they were offered at her door did not necessarily mean she would actually use them. In fact, poor rural populations often see larger families in a logical calculus that more children equals more sons equals more labor equals greater income equals more savings equals a greater land base equals greater old-age security and a better life overall. To use contraceptives then becomes an invitation to a poorer quality of life. Nonetheless, despite the absence of any measurable downward movement in fertility, the Harvard researchers interpreted the high rates of contraceptive acceptance in the Khanna Study as success. According to Mamdani, the lack of face validity in their dependent variable arose from the research team's erroneous presumption that reduced fertility was desired by the study population.[19]

The desire to avoid similar problems, especially socio-economic differentiation, generated efforts that focused explicitly on maximizing participation as a means to the end of development. A classic example here is Bangladesh's Grameen Bank. Unlike the Green Revolution, poverty and landlessness are practical requirements for participation in the Grameen Bank's micro-lending program.[20] These requirements effectively eliminate those lacking the basic need, thus reducing differentiation. Another practical requirement for the borrower is a personal reputation for meeting social and familial obligations, a quality of character believed indicative of the likelihood of also meeting financial obligations otherwise borne by fellow participants. What for and how the borrowed capital is to be used is partly a group participatory decision, but ultimately a small-scale, individual household-level decision.[21] Weakness in such social relations has more recently been recognized as a major factor in unsuccessful cases of micro-finance.[22]

The Grameen Bank further appears to recognize lessons from history that suggest certain cultural patterns are more conducive to overcoming poverty than others.[23] This recognition is embodied in the Sixteen Decisions and the Four Principles, requirements placed upon all borrowers from the Bank.[24] Significant among the Four Principles are admonitions for self-discipline and hard work. Among the Decisions are agreements to keep families small, to refuse to give or accept dowry, and to educate the individual borrower and all the household's children, both male and female. There are other Decisions requiring the borrower to protect the household's health and labor productivity by using clean water, practicing sanitation, and cultivating a vegetable garden to improve diet and produce goods for sale and subsequent savings.[25] If taken together, the capital provided through loans and these Principles and Decisions would tend to provide an efficient use of the small borrowed increments to capital stock, improve technical and organizational skills, teach economizing behavior, raise educational levels, improve health, and open greater choices to those who have long had few.[26]

In addition to those households lacking the landlessness or poverty needed to make micro-lending attractive, non-participants in Grameen's micro-lending also include those lacking the personal reputation needed to make character an adequate substitute for collateral[27] and those unwilling to make the behavioral changes represented by the Sixteen Decisions and Four Principles. Taken together, this dual have-and-have-not nature of non-participation in a local, small-scale development effort like the Grameen Bank suggests that whatever level of participation is achieved is the right level; that is, development assistance is limited to those who need the assistance and those who will (rather than can) make use of it. This makes it easy to define participation itself as success in rural development.[28] This effective definition of success has generated a body of practical[29] and instructional[30] literature in rural development concerned with a variety of "participatory" tools[31] and approaches[32] in development efforts. This is particularly true when those efforts are associated with a local or regional natural resource base.[33]

"Participation" is another frequent topic of original research, statistical analysis of existing census and other survey data, and especially discussion and commentary pieces in the academic and professional literature of rural development. A survey of on-line social science, natural science, and general academic bibliographic abstracting services indicated that since the mid-1980s several hundred refereed and other articles have been published in which "participation" combined with "development", "rural development", "economic development", "resource development", "resource conservation", or "resource management" is a key term. Roughly one-sixth of this "participation" literature presents original research data. These data were collected from "participating communities," "participating households," or individual and groups of "female participants." Not one refereed or other article could be identified from these same on-line services when "non-participation" was substituted for "participation" as the basic key term. Within the "participation" literature presenting original research data, non-participants were included in the data collection only if households or individuals were randomly sampled, but were usually eliminated from further data collection once they were identified as non-participants.[34] Taken as a whole, this literature indicates by their omission that one group of non-participants, the poorest of the poor, and their quality of life continue to be ignored in the field of rural development.

This omission was all the motivation needed for me to follow my student and study non-participation in rural assistance efforts. It also helped that this topic could be studied among the Portuguese-speaking people of the many small villages of rural Minas Gerais, the stomping grounds of my days in the Peace Corps more than twenty years before.

NOTES

1. Sue Branford and Jan Rocha. 2002. *Cutting the Wire: The Story of the Landless Movement in Brazil* (London: Latin American Bureau, 2002): 148–208.

2. José F. de Camargo, *Exodo Rural do Brasil* (Rio de Janeiro: Editora Conquista, 1960).

3. Germán Cutz, 1997. *Reasons for Non-Participation of Adults in Rural Literacy Programs in Western Guatemala* (Ed.D dissertation, Department of Adult Education, Teacher's College, Ball State University, 1997). See also Germán Cutz and Paul Chandler, "Nonparticipation of Mayan Adults in Rural Literacy Programs," *Convergence* 32, no. 1–4 (1999); "The Etic-Emic Conflict of Adult Education: Promoting Literacy of Loss of Cultural Identity," *Education as Change* 3, no. 1 (June 1999); and "Emic-Etic Conflicts as Explanation of Nonparticipation in Adult Education among the Maya of Western Guatemala," *Adult Education Quarterly* 51, no. 1 (November 2000).

4. ———, *Reasons for Non-Participation of Adults*, 113–115.

5. ——, *Reasons for Non-Participation of Adults*, 116–119.

6. ——, *Reasons for Non-Participation of Adults*, 119–123.

7. ——, *Reasons for Non-Participation of Adults*, 124–127.

8. World Resources Institute (WRI), *Participatory Rural Appraisal Handbook: Conducting PRAs in Kenya* (New York: World Resources Institute Center for International Development and Environment, 1991), 1.

9. Terry D. Bergdall, *Methods for Active Participation: Experiences in Rural Development from East and Central Africa* (Nairobi: Oxford University Press, 1993), 6.

10. Luis Flores Quiros, "The Community Enterprise and Peasant Participation," *Desarrollo en las Americas* 6, no. 3 (September 1974): 77–95.

11. Cathy Nesmith, "Gender, Trees, and Fuel: Social Forestry in West Bengal, India," *Human Organization* 50, no. 4 (Winter 1991): 337–348.

12. Robert Chambers, *Rural Development: Putting the Last First* (Essex, UK: Longman Scientific and Technical, 1983).

13. Cutz, *"Reasons for Non-Participation of Adults*, 41–42.

14. Norman Borlaug, "The Green Revolution: For Bread and Peace," *Bulletin of the Atomic Scientists* 27, no. 3 (June, 1971): 6–9, 42–48.

15. Chris Dixon, *Rural Development in the Third World* (London: Routledge, 1990), 38–41.

16. Mike Parnwell, *Population Movements and the Third World* (London: Routledge, 1993), 5–6, 82.

17. Mahmood Mamdani, *The Myth of Population Control: Family, Caste, and Class in an Indian Village* (New York: Monthly Review Press, 1972).

18. John B. Wyons and John E. Gordon, *The Khanna Study: Population Problems in the Rural Punjab* (Cambridge, MA: Harvard University Press, 1971).

19. Mamdani, *The Myth of Population Control*, 30–31, 42.

20. Abu N.M. Wahid, "The Socioeconomic Conditions of Bangladesh and the Evolution of the Grameen Bank," in *The Grameen Bank: Poverty Relief in Bangladesh*, ed. Abu N.M. Wahid (Boulder, CO: Westview Press, Inc., 1993), 3–5.

21. Mahabub Hossain, "The Grameen Bank: Its Origins, Organization, and Management Style," in *The Grameen Bank: Poverty Relief in Bangladesh*, ed. Abu N.M. Wahid (Boulder, CO: Westview Press, Inc.), 13–15.

22. Michael J.V. Woolcock, "Learning from Failures in Microfinance: What Unsuccessful Cases tell us about how Group-Based Programs Work," *The American Journal of Economics and Sociology* 58, no. 1 (January 1999): 17–36.

23. Rondo Cameron, "Economic Development: Some Lessons from History," *American Economic Review* 57, no. 2 (May 1967): 312–324.

24. See note 21 above.

25. Hossain, "The Grameen Bank," 15–16.

26. Wahid, "The Socioeconomic Conditions of Bangladesh," 5–6.

27. See note 22 above.

28. João Maros Alem and Leda Maria Benevello de Castro, "Peasant Participation in an Integrated Rural Development Program, Minas Gerais, Brazil," *Research in Rural Sociology and Development* 3 (1987): 43–64.

29. Robert Chambers, "The Origins and Practice of Participatory Rural Appraisal," *World Development* 22, no 7 (July 1994): 953–969.

30. WRI, *Participatory Rural Appraisal Handbook: Conducting PRAs in Kenya* (New York: World Resources Institute Center for International Development and Environment, 1991).

31. See note 9 above.

32. John M. Cohen and Norman T. Uphoff, "Participation's Place in Rural Development: Seeking Clarity through Specificity," *World Development* 8, no. 3 (March 1980): 213–235.

33. Program for International Development/National Environment Secretariat (PID/NES), *An Introduction to Participatory Rural Appraisal for Rural Resource Management* (Worcester, UK: Clark University Program for International Development and Nairobi: National Environmental Secretariat, Ministry of Environment and Natural Resources, 1989).

34. Compare to similar survey of research on illiterate and low-literate adults by Cutz, *Reasons for Non-Participation of Adults*, 36–40.

Part Two

VILLAGE LIFE IN THE BUSH ZONE OF MINAS GERAIS

Chapter Eight

A Brief History of Brazil's *Zona da Mata*

Since its independence from Portugal in 1889, Brazil has considered itself "*o país do futuro*," the country of the future.[1] That future never quite seems to arrive, despite the constant dramatic change that all but defines Brazil. This paradox is most visible in Minas Gerais, the inland state where the country's colonial traditions linger in their fullest form. These traditions had their beginnings in the first every-man-for-himself gold rush in the New World.[2]

While murderous *conquistadores* like Cortez, Pizarro, and Coronado were personifications of Spain's genocidal quest for gold, Portugal never mounted comparable expeditions of its own in what became Brazil. Nonetheless, Portugal was hardly innocent of crimes against humanity. Unlike the urban civilizations of Mexico and Peru, Brazil offered the Portuguese no opportunities for immediate plunder, no intensive agrarian cultures to support such a plunder, and only small, scattered, mainly hunter-gatherer populations of Indians to serve as subjects for enslavement.[3] Nonetheless, the quest of the Portuguese in the New World for power and wealth were far more dependent on human chattel slavery than any other nation or empire since the time of the Romans.[4] In the absence of a suitable indigenous American population, the Portuguese turned to Angola, the Guinea coast, and the Congo River delta of Africa for its chattel labor supply.[5] Many Africans taken prisoner in tribal wars, others exchanged to clear local debts, and those captured by Muslim raiders for the explicit purpose of sale into slavery provided an abundance of humans to ship to the New World,[6] despite estimates that half died before reaching the coasts.[7] So great was the demand for labor in Brazil's export sugar economy that, by comparison, for every one African brought in chains to what became the United States at least six and perhaps as many as ten were kidnapped and carried to Brazil.[8] Most of this "black ivory" was sold into

plantation slavery, an invention of the Portuguese,[9] in the coastal Crown cap-
taincies of Bahia, Pernambuco, and Rio de Janeiro for the purpose of producing cane sugar and tobacco, the bases of Brazil's colonial economy.[10]

As these latifundial plantations were sources of significant wealth for Portugal, there was little official concern for the regions beyond these captain-
cies, including the thinly populated, economically primitive inland plateau region of São Paulo de Piratininga.[11] By 1606 the town council of São Paulo
complained to their *donatório*, or lord-proprietor, "Your Worship well knows
that the Portuguese are not hard workers, especially when they are out of their
own country."[12] Four decades later Gaspar Dias Ferreira observed that "the
Portuguese who is overtaken by any misfortune emigrates [to Brazil],"[13] and
other correspondents noted that as soon as these migrants amassed enough
wealth to do so, they acquired a slave to relieve them of the burden of labor.
Boxer wrote that African chattel slaves, "'the hands and feet' of the master,"
were so plentiful that "all but the most impoverished whites relied on slave
labor."[14] This combination of latifundial estates and aversion to work had the
result of no significant smallholder rural economy developing anywhere in
colonial Brazil,[15] including Minas Gerais.[16]

The experience of the Spanish in Mexico and Peru was a further discour-
agement to industry. Many migrants from Portugal held the belief that they
too might "strike it rich" through the discovery of a Brazilian Cibola, the
imagined cities of gold that lured Coronado into the American Southwest, or
another silver-laden Potosí.[17] Such fantasies gave the *bandeiras*, exploratory
expeditions of a few dozen to hundreds of largely mixed blood Euro-Indian
Paulistas,[18] an insatiable wanderlust to roam for months or even years ever
deeper into the *sertão*, the bush country of interior Brazil.[19]

Eventually this roaming achieved its goal, but there is no certainty as to exactly when, exactly where, or exactly to whom it occurred. One account holds
that a *bandeira* in search of the Cataguazes Indians, known to wear golden lip
and ear ornaments, first encountered alluvial gold in the valley of the Rio das
Mortes, today known as the Rio Piranga.[20] Other accounts claim that adven-
turers from Bahia followed the Rio São Francisco upstream through the
sertão to where alluvial gold was discovered in the valley of the Rio das Velhas. All that is certain about this discovery is sometime between 1693 and
1695 at least one *bandeirante* found an outwash of gold along either the Rio
das Mortes, Rio das Velhas, or Rio Doce and that by 1696 the news had
reached Rio de Janeiro, Salvador da Bahia, and Recife in Pernambuco.[21] Another certainty is that the quantity of gold exceeded anything ever encountered by the Spanish *conquistadores*.[22]

The news of gold "free for the taking" had the same effect in both Portugal and colonial Brazil that it later had in California, Australia, and Alaska.

Migrants who had once worked only long enough to purchase a slave now did so to purchase a horse or mule.[23] Even priests and friars were so overcome by the lust for gold that the Crown felt it necessary to ban the creation of new religious orders in the region. Gold seekers followed numerous routes to the gold fields, none of which offered easy going. They could leave Rio de Janeiro and struggle northward to the Campos Gerais, the gap between the treacherous Serra da Mantiqueira and the equally rugged Serra do Espinhaço and hope they were not set upon by any remnant bands of the deadly Cataguazes. Or from Bahia or Pernambuco they could either take the south-westerly route along the Rio São Francisco to the headwaters of the Rio das Velhas, a far longer but much less arduous journey, or descend the coast until meeting the Rio Jequitinonha, ascend that river as far as possible, then trek directly overland through the barren Serra do Frio.[24]

By any of these routes, unless they were on the highest slopes, the trekkers were confronted by the densely intertwined *mata*, the heavy tropical and subtropical forests that choked all the region's valleys down to the very edges of the rivers and streams. So thick were these forests that there are accounts from the early days in the gold fields of four days being required to travel the twelve kilometers from Villa Rica de Ouro Prêto to Ribeirão do Carmo, later known as Ouro Prêto and Mariana, respectively.[25]

Once in the gold fields, the prospectors were confronted by many other challenges. The first and often simplest of these was to find the gold itself. At the beginning of the rush this could be done with the naked eye as the gold glittered from beneath the rivers and streams in what were called *faisqueiras*, a term derived from the verb *faiscar*, to sparkle, twinkle, or glitter. When the rainy season made this method both difficult and dangerous, prospectors would explore the *taboleiros*, the narrow flats along the banks of the watercourses. When these easy pickings were exhausted or all the other promising sites were occupied, the *guapiaras*, the clefts in the stone of the steep hillsides, were explored. As long as these forms of extraction were possible, prospectors would need little more than a *bateia*, or gold pan.[26]

Discovering a lucrative site created the next, potentially deadly challenge, this time from other prospectors who might simply trespass on the site or, if accompanied by armed slaves, expel or kill the original claimant. According to the Governor-General of Bahia, such bold and frequent crimes by the "vagabond and base people, low-class and immoral," were punished only by vengeance, if at all.[27]

By the summer of 1697–98 and again in the summer of 1700–01, the miners had brought upon themselves yet another mortal challenge wholly of their own making. Early in the 18th Century Antonil noted "the land which yields gold is exceedingly barren of all that is necessary for human life."[28] And as few of the prospectors would take time away from their *bateias* to plant or tend even the hardiest of crops such as maize or manioc, they were soon faced with famine. At times the situation became so desperate that miners and slaves alike were forced to abandon the search for gold and forage for anything edible that could be found in the *mata*. So great was the crisis that a dog or cat for the table would fetch two ounces of gold.[29]

In hopes of bringing order to the region and reducing the violence, the Portuguese Crown attempted to implement a number of largely useless regulatory policies. Among these was a limit of 200 slaves that could be brought into the region, but the demand for chattel labor was so much greater in the gold region that ships arriving with this human cargo often diverted from the sugar ports of Recife and Salvador da Bahia to Rio de Janeiro where buyers paid much higher prices in gold.[30] The same was true with cattle. Although the animals usually arrived in very poor condition, the prices paid justified driving them along the Rio São Francisco or across the Serra do Frio and brought regular crises in the food supply to the less profitable markets in Pernambuco and Bahia.[31]

"Without any kind of well-ordered government,"[32] the only reasonably successful policy was the establishment of the system of *datas de ouro* mining claims. As summarized by Boxer, each complete *data* measuring 30 square *braças*, or arm lengths, was divided into fourths. The first successful prospector in any given place had the right to choose for himself the first two *datas*, while the third was allotted directly to the Crown, which regularly and immediately sold it to the highest bidder, and the fourth to the *Guarda-Mór*, the Crown's local representative. All the remaining *datas* in the immediate vicinity were allocated by drawing lots, their ultimate size being determined at a rate of two square *braças* for each slave a miner would employ. In the districts where the *datas* were not subject to such official distribution, unless otherwise seized by violence or intimidation, ownership of any given gold-bearing site was established by prior possession. In Ouro Prêto these unofficial claims were known as the "General Mines," the origin of the name Minas Gerais that was applied to the region beyond and including the Serra do Espinhaço.[33]

Eventually the gold of Minas Gerais was played out. After a few decades the alluvial deposits were exhausted and tunnel-and-shaft mines operated by slaves replaced them. Within another half-century these deposits were also mined out and by the first decade of the 19th Century gold mining in southern Minas Gerais was all but over.[34] Reflections of the immense wealth of Brazil's "Golden Age" may be seen today in the 23 magnificent Baroque churches of Ouro Prêto and in other equally and in some cases even more spectacular churches in Mariana, São João del Rei, Congonhas do Campo,

Sabará, Tiradentes, and other *Cidades de Ouro* less frequently visited by the mainly European tourists of today seeking the diversions and dissipations of Brazil's world famous *Carnaval*.

Also gone by this time were the lush forests that had so plagued the early gold seekers and given the southeastern corner of Minas Gerais its now oxymoronic name of *Zona da Mata*, the bush zone. The forests were taken down for a number of reasons. One was the practice of slash-and-burn agriculture, or *roça* as it known in Brazil. As the soil in this part of Minas Gerais was unsuited to agriculture,[35] the rotation between each episode of slashing and burning was much too short for the forest to recover and re-establish itself by natural means. The pigs and chickens that comprised most of the early settlers' livestock also contributed by being allowed to forage on the loose, so the seed needed to regenerate the forests were often devoured as soon as they hit the ground. Cutting fuelwood for cooking as well as gold smelting further subjected the forests to continuing removals from which they could not recover. Altogether, these activities have resulted in a landscape largely devoid of trees. Today travelers from the south to Ouro Prêto can have broad, even beautiful vistas all the way to the southern end of the Serra do Espinhaço that are obstructed only by the scrub brush on a few hilltops or the occasional row of bamboo marking property boundaries between the small farms and ranches situated in region's valleys. Outside the few national and state parks, the overwhelming majority of what forests exist in Minas Gerais are extensive plantations of exotics, usually the eucalypts grown for rendering into the charcoal needed for metal smelting by the vertically integrated steel companies in fossil fuel poor Brazil.

As for the people of the *Zona da Mata*, the relationships between the have and have-not classes remain much as they were during the gold rush. Unlike the sugar-growing regions of Bahia and Pernambuco, Minas Gerais was not dominated by the *sesmarias*, the large land grants from the Crown,[36] although *fazendas* of a few dozen to several hundred hectares can be found surrounding the small towns and villages that dot the region. As in the colonial days, these *fazendas* continue to have primarily an export orientation, producing coffee, sugar and beef for the international market and dairy products for the larger towns and cities within Minas Gerais and other states.[37] The *padrões*, owners of the larger *fazendas*, often play prominent if not dominant roles in both the social and political structure of the rural *municípios*,[38] political units equivalent to counties in the United States. Since the end of Brazil's military directly controlling the government in 1989, free voting and laws forbidding office holders to succeed themselves have eliminated the unbroken political dominance of individual *fazendeiros* in the rural areas of Minas Gerais. Still, the patronage these men (very rarely women) have to give or to withhold insures that Brazil's colonial patriarchal social structure will continue for many years to come.[39] The hold of the have families is further reinforced by their habits of intermarriage and avoidance of racial mixing.[40] Families of non-African descent with lesser landholdings are particularly averse to "diluting" their stock.[41]

For the have-nots, particularly if they are of African descent, opportunities are severely limited. In some cases diligence, cleverness, and family unity can result in the ownership of a *sítio*, the small landholdings of a few *litros* (one hectare equals sixteen *litros*) of tillable soil that have long been Brazil's subsistence truck farms, but the vast majority of the rural poor are landless.[42] In the rural areas of Minas Gerais, the poor are often welcomed as squatters as they constitute a captive labor supply, either through traditional family-to-family sharecropping and tenancy arrangements or, more often today, sub-minimum wage labor.[43] The seasonal gardens they cultivate in the *quintal* that surrounds each home provides a diet of starchy root crops such as beets, turnips, carrots, and onions and a few hardy vegetables like okra and collards. Most of their protein comes from the eggs produced by the chickens they allow to forage wherever they will, the means to cage and feed them daily being an economic impossibility. Under such conditions, it is to be expected that Brazil has an infant mortality rate exceeded on the continent only by Bolivia and Guyana and that its life expectancy is the third lowest.[44]

The have-and-have-not disparity is further perpetuated by Brazil's education system. The *cidade*, the central "city" from which each rural *município* is governed, usually has some form of school, but the pay and the quality of preparation the teachers receive is quite low. Rural schools also rarely offer more than four to six years of education, just enough to provide the most basic literacy. By the end of the 20th Century only Bolivia had a lower literacy rate in South America than Brazil.[45] Rather than subject their children to these schools, those with the means will send their children to private schools. If a family aspires to give any of their children a university education, upon graduation from secondary school a promising youth will be enrolled in a private *curso pre-vestibular*, a yearlong preparatory program to train young people to pass the rigorous national *vestibular* entrance exam. However, once the child has succeeded in gaining admission to a public university, the tuition, fees, and often room and board are free. If the college graduate has shown some ability, has the connections, or usually both, they may even be admitted to a graduate program that provides them a salary of several multiples of the national *salário mínimo*, in addition to the free tuition and fees. Individuals from poor, rural, unconnected families rarely break through this rigid social and economic structure without the ability or lack of scruples needed to manipulate others to their advantage. One of the significant results of this elitist education system is that the rural poor take a distant second place to the environment;[46] hence, such phenomena as the green tree laws that greatly contribute to the squalid living conditions of the Kaïngang Indians described in the preceding chapter.

A further reinforcement to the rigid social, political, and economic structure of rural Brazil is the Catholic Church. Despite the voluminous writing about "liberation theology" and "progressive" priests that have been staples of academics addressing Latin America since the 1960s,[47] the rural priesthood in Minas Gerais is almost entirely under the sway of the *padrões* and their interrelated families.[48] In the face of such a thoroughgoing rigidity, the rural-to-urban exodus occurring throughout the developing world has not bypassed Brazil's *Zona da Mata*. In 1970 the population of the Zona da Mata was almost exactly evenly split between urban and rural locales. Twenty years later, almost three-fourths of the people lived in urban areas.[49]

The one domain from which *"o país do futuro"* may actually and finally emerge appears to be religion. Like much of Africa, parts of South Asia, and the rest of Latin America,[50] Brazil is undergoing a rapid flowering of evangelical, especially Pentecostal, Protestantism.[51] From at most three or four percent of the total population in 1960, evangelicals were estimated to account for just over twenty percent by the end of the 20th Century.[52] According to Levine, "By 1997, sixteen million Brazilian *crentes* (believers) followed daily practices—austerity in dress, abstention from alcohol, a fierce Puritanism—that represented the antithesis of Brazil's historical popular culture. . . . The Pentecostal explosion has deeply affected its followers, instilling a disciplined work ethic that has produced astonishing gains in earning power for its members, most of them from the poorest social groups."[53]

While Levine's comments on "daily practices" are plainly visible in the urban areas of Minas Gerais, the rural areas remain bastions not just of Brazil's colonial social traditions, but the conservatism of its religious history. In 1999 this religious transformation did not appear of sufficient magnitude in rural Minas Gerais to constitute a conflating variable in a study of reasons for non-participation in rural assistance efforts. For this reason, and in view of the history, society, and culture of the region, my research sought to test the hypothesis that participation in rural assistance would be positively correlated with measures of poor health, economic need, and demographic tragedy; that is, if a suitable project could be designed, a better life could be brought to the poorest of Brazil's rural poor. The challenge would be identifying and designing that suitable project.

NOTES

1. Hernane Tavares da Sá, *The Brazilians: People of Tomorrow* (New York: Praeger, 1947).

2. Robert M. Levine, *The History of Brazil* (Westport, CT: Greenwood Press, 1999), 48–51.

3 Boris Fausto, *A Concise History of Brazil*, trans. by Arthur Brakel (Cambridge: Cambridge University Press, 1999), 6–9.

4. Levine, *The History of Brazil*, 30–33, 34–37, 46.

5. ——, *The History of Brazil*, 42.

6. Adam Hochschild, *Bury the Chains: Prophets and Rebels in the Fight to Free an Empire's Slaves* (New York: Houghton Mifflin, 2005).

7. Caio Prado, Jr., *Formação do Brasil Contemporâneo Colônia* (São Paulo: Editôra Brasiliense, 1963), 91–92. See also Levine, *The History of Brazil*, 46–48.

8. C.R. Boxer, *The Golden Age of Brazil, 1695–1750: Growing Pains of a Colonial Society* (Berkeley, CA: University of California Press, 1962), 2–7. See also Howard A. Zinn, *A People's History of the United States* (New York: Harper Perennial, 1980), 49.

9. Jim Goad, *The Redneck Manifesto* (New York: Simon & Schuster, 1997), 216–217.

10. James Lang, *Portuguese Brazil: The King's Plantation* (New York: Academic Press, 1979), 142–145. Also see Prado, *Formação do Brasil*, 148–179.

11. Boxer, *The Golden Age of Brazil*, 31–32.

12. Cited in Boxer, *The Golden Age of Brazil*, 33.

13. Cited in Boxer, *The Golden Age of Brazil*, 10.

14. Boxer, *The Golden Age of Brazil*, 2.

15. Shepard Forman, *The Brazilian Peasantry* (New York: Columbia University, 1975), 20.

16. Laird W. Bergad, *Slavery and the Demographic and Economic History of Minas Gerais, Brazil, 1720–1888* (Cambridge: Cambridge University Press, 1999), 26–80.

17. Boxer, *The Golden Age of Brazil*, 35.

18. Lang, *Portuguese Brazil*, 123–124.

19. Levine, *The History of Brazil*, 45–46.

20. See note 17 above.

21. Fausto, *A Concise History of Brazil*, 49.

22. Lang, *Portuguese Brazil*, 125.

23. Fausto, *A Concise History of Brazil*, 49–50.

24. Boxer, *The Golden Age of Brazil*, 39–41, 53–54.

25. ——, *The Golden Age of Brazil*, 37.

26. Lang, *Portuguese Brazil*, 126–127.

27. Cited in Boxer, *The Golden Age of Brazil*, 41.

28. João Antonio Andreoni Antonil, *Cultura e Opulência do Brasil* (1711 edition reprinted by São Paulo: Compania Editora Nacional, 1967), 372.

29. Boxer, *The Golden Age of Brazil*, 47–48.

30. Antonil, *Cultura e Opulência do Brasil*, 370.

31. Levine, *The History of Brazil*, 50–51.

32. Antonil, *Cultura e Opulência do Brasil,* 368.

33. Boxer, *The Golden Age of Brazil,* 51–52.

34. Fausto, *A Concise History of Brazil*, 53.

35. Prado, *Formação do Brasil*, 54.

36. Forman, *The Brazilian Peasantry*, 22–27, 30–31.

37. Prado, *Formação do Brasil*, 265–270.

38. Paulo R. Schilling, *Brasil de los Latifundistas,* (Montevideo: Editorial Dialogo R.S.L., 1967), 76–80.

39. Gilberto Freyre, "The Patriarchal Basis of Brazilian Society," in *Politics of Change in Latin America,* eds. Joseph Maier and Richard W. Weatherhead (New York: Praeger, 1964), 77–98.

40. Charles Wagley, *An Introduction to Brazil* (revised edition) (New York: Columbia University Press, 1971), 52–53, 168–174.

41. Gilberto Freyre, *The Masters and Slaves: A Study in the Development of Brazilian Civilization,* trans. by Samuel Putnam (New York: Praeger, 1946).

42. Levine, *The History of Brazil*, 164–166.

43. Sebastião Araújo de Oliveira, *Plano Municipal de Saúde* (Senhora de Oliveira, MG: Copiadora Pirangense, 1996).

44. Population Reference Bureau, *2004 World Population Data Sheet* (Washington: Population Reference Bureau, 2004), 7–8.

45. See note 44 above. Also see Armin K. Ludwig, *Brazil: A Handbook of Historical Statistics* (Boston: G.K. Hall & Co., 1985), 132.

46. Levine, *The History of Brazil*, 152.

47. ———, *The History of Brazil*, 149.

48. Wagley, *An Introduction to Brazil*, 167–185.

49. Instituto Brasileiro de Geografia e Economia (IBGE), *Senso Demográfico de 1990* (Rio de Janeiro: Instituto Brasileiro de Geografia e Economia, 1991).

50. Philip Jenkins, *The Next Christendom: The Coming Global Christianity* (Oxford: Oxford University Press, 2003).

51. Patrick Johnstone, *Operation World: The Day-to-Day Guide to Praying for the World* (Grand Rapids: Zondervan Publishing House, 1995), 62.

52. ———, *Operation World*, 128–130.

53. Levine, *The History of Brazil*, 26.

Chapter Nine

The Ethics of
Research in Rural Development

The search for research opportunities in Costa Rica and Rio Grande do Sul, in addition to being fruitless and depressing, brought a new perspective to my efforts in rural development. The idea of traveling to poor and isolated communities and leaving with data and experiences that might be of benefit to my life had become an insufficient motivation. If my presence in these communities was to be justifiable, any future efforts must also leave a lasting improvement in the quality of life for the local population that supposedly is the goal of the type of effort I wanted to realize. From this perspective, the knowable, albeit unintended, consequence of dependency resulting from a "redistribution of wealth" from my pocket to those of the less fortunate, giving a man a fish, as it were, was also unacceptable.

As noted in Chapter 7, "Improving the quality of life in rural communities is a primary goal of development,"[1] but if that goal is to be achieved, then the assumption that "rural people can be agents of their own development"[2] must become a reality. This means that not only must a man be taught to fish, as the parable goes, but that man must also apply himself to learning to fish. Or as John Bolt of the Calvin Theological Seminary has observed, "the poor have some responsibility for getting out of poverty," so "we must honor . . . poor people and give them the full dignity of responsible stewardship."[3]

This means that the practical goal of the research in Brazil, improving the quality of life in a poor rural community in the *Zona da Mata* of Minas Gerais, had to be the presentation of an opportunity for the poor themselves to realize that goal.[4] This necessarily carries the assumption that the people of such a community desire an improvement in their quality of life. It further means that such an improvement in the quality of life must have universal emic relevance to these people; that is, it must be something that *everyone* in the community sees as useful, necessary, and lacking (see discussion of the emic-etic distinction in Chapter 4). And since my time in Brazil, in part, had been purchased through a successful application for a Fulbright scholarship to pursue teaching and research in agroforestry, the improvement in quality of life ultimately had to take form in some way agricultural or silvicultural. By themselves, these two conditions promised to be a challenge.

Unlike the seemingly unending challenges of my earlier work in China, the intended work in Brazil offered significant certainties. The first certainty was the knowledge of the power of the beauty of Ouro Prêto and the other Cities of Gold to distract me should frustrations arise, which was also a certainty. The second was the certainty of a letter of invitation provided by Dr. Laércio Couto, my former counterpart during my days in the Peace Corps and now a full professor at the Federal University of Viçosa in Minas Gerais. By my having agreed in writing to teach his assigned courses and maintain his on-going cooperative industrial research projects, Dr. Couto had been able to leave his job in 1976 and travel to Canada for a doctorate in forestry. When he first made the suggestion of a Fulbright scholarship to come teach a course in agroforestry at Viçosa, I knew with further certainty what to expect: Once again, I would be doing at least part of his job. In exchange, he offered the services of his three graduate students in any research efforts I might be able to mount in the field of agroforestry. Learning of my current interests in participation, Laércio further tempted me with the fact the doctoral candidate among the three graduate students had some experience in using the partici-patory methods developed by Chambers in Africa.[5] It all seemed too easy and too good to be true, and of course it was.

POVERTY IN THE VALLEY OF THE DEAD

Fernandinho, or "Little Fernando," the doctoral student under Dr. Couto's su-pervision, simplified the process of identifying a suitable site to realize the goals of this research. At the time he was working under a grant from the World Wildlife Fund to measure the ecological benefits of incorporating trees into several coffee plantations in the *Zona da Mata*. Two of his field sites were located in the *município* of Senhora de Oliveira, a poor rural county sit-uated in the upper portions of the watershed of the Rio Piranga, known dur-ing Brazil's colonial era as the Rio das Mortes, the River of the Dead. Both of these sites were owned by a former *prefeito* (mayor) of the *município*, a man known locally as Tiãozinho, or "Little Sebastian." In addition to his political prominence, Little Sebastian, was by far the largest landowner in the *município*, its most significant *padrão*, and its only college graduate.

According to Little Fernando, my research would be appealing to Little Sebastian because he was "*bem progressivo*," very progressive, "*bem interesado
no meio-ambiente*," very interested in the environment, and hoping once
again to be elected *prefeito* after the mandatory no-repeats limitation on oc-
cupying public office had passed. Little Sebastian was, in fact, quite interested in the research, especially as my intention to bring an immediately tangible benefit to the local populace would be a definite plus in his re-election
hopes. After learning the conditions of a suitable research site, Little Sebastian suggested a community called Prudentes, the village of his birth.

Suitability required several conditions. Most broadly, the site had to present aggregate conditions of poverty and landlessness exceeding comparable
existing measures of such conditions within the *Zona da Mata*. These conditions included low household income levels, a concentrated distribution of
landholding, an on-going rural-to-urban migration, lack of physical infrastructure, low levels of education, a high agricultural percent within the distribution of employment, subsistence crops giving way to cash crop dominance within the community's crop mix, and high rates of morbidity and
mortality among the people. Prudentes, a collection of fourteen rural hamlets
dispersed along the drainage of the Ribeirão das Almas (Map 9.1), a tributary
of the Rio Piranga, met all these depressing conditions.

Little Sebastian provided aggregate economic statistics from the early to
mid 1990s for the *município* as a whole (Table 9.1), which included the community of Prudentes. One immediately notices that most of the population received "up to one minimum salary," which begs the question of whether the
term "minimum salary" has any meaning within the rural Brazilian context.
Equally depressing aggregate health indicators (Table 9.2) were also provided
for the *município* as a whole as well as for the small *cidade* of Senhora de
Olivera itself.

My own observations, the accounts of the current agents of state rural technical assistance (EMATER) and public health posts in Senhora de Oliveira
and Prudentes, and that of the current lay *ministro* of the Catholic Church in
Prudentes all shared the view that poverty and landlessness were both *mais
comúm* (more common) and *mais problemática* (more problematic) in Prudentes than in either the *cidade* of Senhora de Oliveira or the *município* as a
whole.

As with the health statistics for Senhora de Oliveira, the statistics on rural-ur-
ban population distribution (Table 9.3) can be misleading unless one keeps in
mind that the 45.5 percent "urban" population of the *cidade* of Senhora de
Oliveira totaled only 2317 persons in 1990. By contrast, urban areas within the
larger *Zona da Mata* of Minas Gerais include numerous transportation, commercial, light industrial, and tourist centers of populations in the tens of thou-

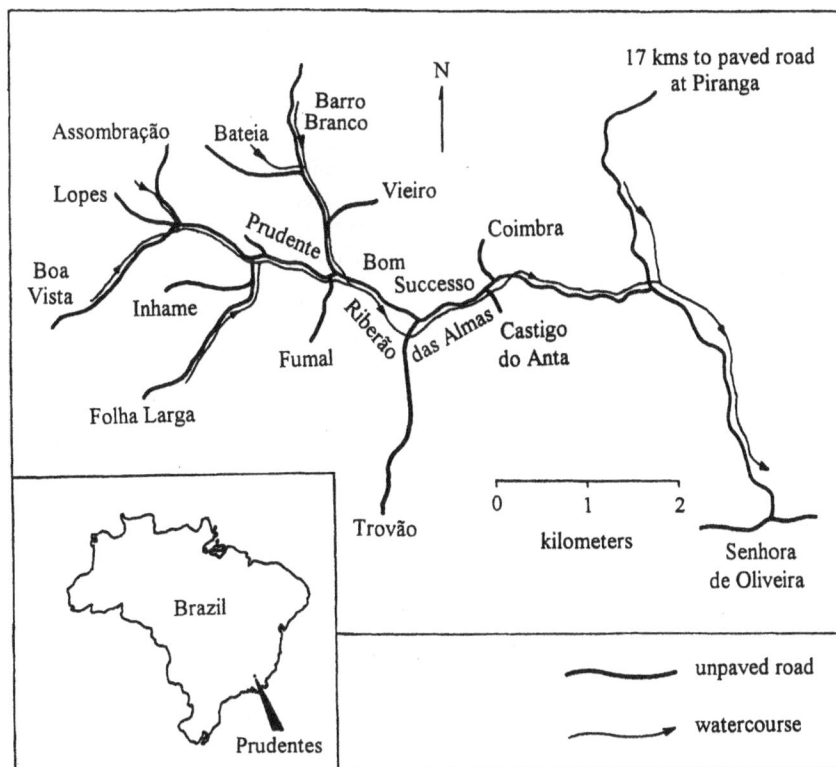

Map 9.1. The fourteen hamlets of Prudentes, the municipio of Senhora de Oliveira, and their approximate location within Brazil (inset).

sands, plus the hundreds of thousands in Juiz de Fora, a major regional business, manufacturing, and governmental hub in the southeast part of the state. Senhora de Oliveira is, has been, and is likely to remain more agrarian than the *Zona da Mata* as a whole. The youth of its population is also understated by the age distribution statistics due to on-going, although apparently slowing, high crude birth rates and an on-going, apparently accelerating, out-migration that draws mainly those in their teens and twenties to the large industrial metropolis of Belo Horizonte, the capital of Minas Gerais, to Juiz de Fora, and to other much smaller cities and towns in the southeastern part of the state.

By all critical measures of economics, health, and its decidedly rural character, Prudentes appeared entirely suitable for both the goals of the research and the goal leaving behind a tangible improvement in the community's quality of life. Unfortunately, neither Little Sebastian nor Little Fernando shared more than tangential interests in the bigger goals that were the source of my own motivation.

Table 9.1. Economic Statistics for Município of Senhora de Oliveira, including Prudentes

Agricultural Land Use (1994):

Subsistence crops:	(ha.)	Cash crops:	(ha.)
maize	730	Eucalyptus spp.	920
brown beans (1st)	200	sugarcane	800
brown beans (2nd)	75	coffee	40
dry rice	35	Citrus spp.	12
irrigated rice	1	bananas	4
manioc	1		
potatoes	1		
dairy pasturage	110		

Domestic Livestock (1993):		Adult Literacy Rate (1994):	
cattle	4500	4th grade level only	46.8%
swine	1910	8th grade level	19.2%
goats	65	12th grade level	2.4%
chickens	13500		
horses	410		
mules	35		

		Household Income	
Employment by Sector (1990):		Distribution (1996):	
agricultural	64.3%	up to 1 minimum salary	93.82%
industrial	11.5%	1 to 3 minimum salaries	4.51%
commercial	2.6%	3 to 5 minimum salaries	1.09%
transport and storage	3.6%	over 5 minimum salaries	0.58%
other services	17.0%		

Source: Oliveira, 1996[6]

Table 9.2. Health Statistics for *Município* of Senhora de Oliveira, including Prudentes

Selected Health Indicators (1996):
    #1 fatal disease: arterial hypertension
    #1 chronic disease: water-borne parasites
    average fecal coliform: 200 colonies per 100ml water
    adult periodontal disease rate >> 35%
    children without personal toothbrush > 60%

Available Sewage Facilities (1996):

System type	Urban %	Rural %
public net	84.6	27.0
irrigated cesspool	1.6	16.7
dry cesspool	12.0	32.7
"open heaven"	1.8	23.6

Annual Percent Mortality (1993–96):

General	0.70
Infant	3.75

Source: Oliveira, 1996[7]

Table 9.3. Population Distribution

Spatial Distribution (1990):

Year	Senhora de Oliveira			Zona da Mata	
	Total	Urban	Rural	Urban	Rural
1970	4742	27.5%	72.5%	49.3%	50.7%
1980	4812	36.5%	64.5%	60.6%	39.4%
1990	5132	45.5%	54.5%	72.8%	27.2%

Age Distribution (1990):

Age class	Senhora de Oliveira	Zona da Mata
0–14	30.5%	26.8%
15–30	31.0%	31.3%
31–50	21.0%	22.6%
50+	17.5%	19.3%

Sources: Oliveira 1996[8]; Franco 1995[9]; IBGE 1991[10]

NON-PARTICIPATION IN PARTICIPATORY METHODS

As the research was intended to be an applied study of participation and non-participation in rural assistance, its focus was on those households that seemed by their non-participation to defy the assumption that rural people can be the agents of their development. The social science goals of the work were twofold.

The primary goal was the generation of hypotheses to guide future work through the elicitation, verification, and analysis of reasons reported by rural households for not participating in a minimal labor, no-cash-cost, broad time-window rural assistance project. Basically similar qualitative methods for data collection and analysis that had been used in my earlier research in China (see Chapter 4) could be used in Prudentes to pursue this goal. The secondary goal was the determination of possible distinguishing statistical differences in the economic and health characteristics of participating and non-participating households identified through realization of the primary goal. Quantitative methods could be used to pursue this goal. In both cases, Little Fernando's experience with the participatory methods of Chambers,[11] Kapoor,[12] and others[13] seemed to be the most appropriate path to follow as soon as my obligations for teaching a five-week graduate course in agro-forestry had been fulfilled.

At my request, Little Fernando contacted Little Sebastian to schedule a meeting at the Prudentes Community Center immediately following Mass for the first Sunday after my class had been completed. Little Sebastian agreed to advertise the meeting and have his mother-in-law, the younger sister of the lay *ministro*, request the itinerant priest who served the Catholic Church in the central hamlet of Bom Successo announce the meeting at Mass that morning. On the appointed day, Little Fernando, the two masters students, and I traveled the two hours from Viçosa to Prudentes. After Little Sebastian's brief introduction of the four of us to the attendees, the process began by dividing the group into thirds, each third to be guided separately by one of the three graduate students.

My suspicions were aroused even before our arrival. My earlier time in Brazil, plus the observations of Willems,[14] Costa,[15] Freyre,[16] and other scholars[17] of Brazil all indicated that *parentela*, the extended family of blood, marriage, and adoption, was so all encompassing that civic organization and community-centered efforts are all but unknown in the country. The first sight of that Sunday morning meeting only heightened those suspicions. Of Little Sebastian's estimate of roughly 900 people in the fourteen hamlets of Prudentes, only 47 were in attendance, and those 47 attendees represented only 36 of what were later counted to be a total of 175 households. None of the graduate students shared my worries during the ride back to Viçosa that Sunday afternoon.

By prior arrangement, I returned to Prudentes ten days later and walked the community's dusty roads to begin the process of participant observation.[18] Before noon on the first day back, it was obvious that much of the data collected during the community meeting was seriously flawed. One attendee, the senior male in the hamlet of Vieiro, had vigorously complained that in the past "all the people in Prudentes had gardens, but today at most only ten percent have gardens." Even that morning's superficial exploration of only five hamlets revealed not a single household without a recently harvested summer garden. The winter dry season would begin in six to eight weeks and the gardens of the clearly wealthiest households had already been cleared to receive the seed for a winter crop.

The participatory method dependent on community meetings[19] created another problem. After two days walking the roads with the public health agent, I decided to interview a few households to learn their reasons for not attending the community meeting two weeks earlier. The first interviewee had a good reason for non-participation. The night before he had been shot twice in the head by a drunken friend and had been in a hospital in Belo Horizonte in a deep coma for a week. The next dozen households had equally valid, if less catastrophic reasons. Some said such meetings were a waste of time, which was hardly arguable from what had been learned so far. Others claimed not to have been aware of the meeting, either lacking the literacy to read the posted signs or not attending Mass at the Catholic Church in Bom Successo where it had been announced. While the potential data from this participatory approach were clearly valid, they were equally clearly useless. It seemed that a sampling process was in order.[20]

To this end, beginning on the fourth morning, open-ended interviews were conducted through a sample of 38 of the community's households distributed across all fourteen hamlets. These sampling interviews followed methods designed to make possible analyses of the cognitive domains[21] of (1) the greatest needs of the community and the individual households and (2) possible solutions to those needs. The results of these interviews are summarized in Table 9.4.

While the two greatest problems could not be attacked directly, the third most common problem matched the most frequently cited specific solution of the 38 households and further offered the desired practical improvement in participant households' quality of life. This solution was *"coisas como Zilda trouxe,"* things like Zilda brought. Zilda, a popular former rural technical assistance agent, often had brought packages of freshly or soon-to-be expired garden seed, mainly carrot and beet according to those who specified. As all 38 households interviewed had or had access to existing home gardens and all had at least one year-round water supply, this suggestion offered both the broad applicability needed to identify non-participant households as well as the opportunity to utilize an otherwise idle resource, the winter dry season.

If this idea could be implemented, another possible opportunity seemed to spring from it. In the process of furnishing dry season garden seed and helpful soil amendments, the households of Prudentes could be offered the opportunity to prepare to receive fruit tree seedlings available to me, as a member of the Federal University's faculty, at no cost from the state tree nursery

Table 9.4.   Community Needs and Solutions

Community needs and solutions	Households citing
Needs (n = 34 of 38 households offering responses)	
more employment	28
more health assistance	23
winter garden seed	18
more land	14
more fertilizer	9
bigger school	7
better water	6
all others cited twice or less	8
Solutions (n = 27 of 38 households offering responses)	
things like Zilda brought (garden seed)	16
more employment	13
more fertilizer	12
better seed	7
all others cited twice or less	9

Note: Totals exceed n due to multiple responses given by most households

back in Viçosa. The process also created an opportunity to identify landowning households willing to make suitable land available to implant an agroforestry mix of *feijão* (*Phaseolus* sp.), the high-protein brown bean ubiqui-
tous to Brazilian meals, with angicos, locally available, commercially
valuable nitrogen-fixing trees (*Pseudoacacia* spp. and *Piptadenia* spp.) in a
sharecropping system with the landless households of Prudentes. Not only
would the local population benefit from this plan, it would also be sure to satisfy the Fulbright Commission's scholarship requirements as well as Little
Fernando's obsession with putting trees into every ecosystem. Ironically, this
plan only had potential by virtue of a local man named Maxwell, the
EMATER agent who had replaced Zilda. Under the intended conditions of his
job, Maxwell could and should have been doing much of what I intended, but
as a political appointee, he rarely felt it necessary for his shadow to appear
outside his office in Senhora de Oliveira.

Despite the opportunity created by one man's reluctance to do his job, a serious problem with this idea arose nine days later when I returned to Viçosa
and met with Little Fernando and the two masters students to discuss the idea.
While the two masters students seemed open to the plan, Little Fernando
seemed averse to it for three reasons. He made the first reason explicit. He
had no interest in any intermediate steps between his poorly attended community meetings and the implantation of trees, his mission as an environmentalist. The fact that his "environment first" preference was certain to
bring benefits only to the landowning have households of Prudentes, thereby
increasing the already great socio-economic differentiation common to and
ignored within most efforts at rural assistance,[22] was dismissed as the arrogance and ignorance of an imperialist foreigner.

The second reason was implicit from his tightly folded arms, his nervously
agitated body language, and the obvious fear of both of the masters students
at being seen amenable to any idea that did not originate directly from Little
Fernando. At barely over five feet in height, Little Fernando suffered from
chronic "small man syndrome" and helping someone else pursue ideas other
than his own caused him acute attacks of this problem.

The third reason seemed to afflict all three students. As graduate students,
all three were unarguably members of Brazil's have class. The work I proposed would require that we not just drive out to Prudentes for a day, but reside there for many weeks. Worse than the isolation and absence of modern
household conveniences was the strong possibility of returning to Viçosa with
clothes smelling of wood smoke, a marker of members of Brazil's have-not
classes second only to African skin and a point of gossip and ridicule for any
of their peers wishing to slight them.[23] From that point forward, Little Fernando became impossible to work with and every attempt at conversation

brought on episodes of ever increasing agitation and hostility. When offered payment in addition to the twelve minimum salaries he received as a doctoral student, he said he would go back to Prudentes with me, but would not promise to do the work I needed done. Knowing Dr. Couto as well as I did, there was no possibility of a useful intercession on his part.

While I had no problem with doing all the work by myself, which would be considerable, the time limit created by my obligation to return to my job back in the United States meant the initial dry season garden portion of the idea could be realized only with luck. The hypocrisy of those proudly claiming to be *bem progressivo* had never aroused more contempt.

DEVELOPING A PROJECT
THROUGH THE "MORMON METHOD"

Beyond the problem of uncooperative graduate students was one of method. How would the knowledge of the opportunity presented by the project I had in mind be disseminated among the 175 households of Prudentes? The textbook participatory methods, despite their touted efficiencies in labor,[24] were clearly inadequate for the job and the time limitation seemed to rule out any alternatives.

For a week I did little other than wander the sunny hills around Viçosa and stop in for lunch at the Charme, a comfortably dim restaurant with good food and fair beer, while I mulled over my problems. If this effort were doomed to fail before it had even started, at least I would eat well in the meantime. After a few days of this, Bartolomeu Romualdo, the headwaiter at the Charme was naturally curious, especially about a foreigner who spoke Portuguese with a seemingly local *mineiro* accent. He politely intruded to ask a question.

Bartô, as he preferred to be addressed, was a fascinating, well-spoken, and unusually perceptive conversationalist. His education had ended part way through the fourth grade. He had been on his own since the age of eight when his father died and his mother was forced to expel him from their home in Ouro Prêto in favor of raising his two younger sisters on her limited income. He bore no bitterness or ill-will toward her and took great and justly earned pride that he had recently turned forty, was still alive, and was supporting his three-year-son son, his common-law wife, and the son of her earlier companion. He considered himself a *"joaleira tradicional de Ouro Prêto"* as in his teens he had apprenticed himself to a jeweler and learned the craft first created in Brazil during its Golden Age. He also sympathized with my problems of trying to work with both Dr. Couto and the three graduate students and observed, *"Alguém que tenta ajudar os pobres do Brasil já tem bastante problemas*." Anyone who tries to help the poor of Brazil already has enough problems.

One evening after a day spent wandering and talking with Bartô, I told Sherry Ann McNett, a young American woman trying with little success to make some money in Viçosa as a private English tutor, that I wished I could find someone like Bartô to help me with my work.

She had the obvious response, "Why don't you ask Bartô?"

The next day I asked him. He agreed immediately, not waiting to hear what I might offer him as payment. Trying to slow him down at least a little bit, I presented my terms: For each household he interviewed, I would pay him ten Cruzadas, not quite two American dollars. As he earned only 160 Cruzadas per month, it was quite possible that he could earn the equivalent of two months' salary for every two or at most three days we spent in Prudentes just with this initial phase of the work. In addition, for every household that received the garden package or the fruit seedlings, he would receive another ten Cruzadas. And for each household that allowed us to arrange a beans-and-trees sharecropping system, Bartô would earn one hundred Cruzadas. He accepted the terms at once. Relieved to be rid of Little Fernando, I invited Bartô to come to my apartment for dinner a few days later on his day off to begin planning. In the meantime I would try to figure a way to spread the news of the garden seed opportunity to all 175 households in Prudentes in the limited time that would be available to us.

As I was leaving, Bartô told me he had known from the first time we had spoken that God had brought us together for some good reason that would soon enough be revealed. God appeared to be working in other beneficial ways as well.

Among the great changes in Viçosa since my days in the Peace Corps was the presence of a small second-floor Mormon Church in the lower end of downtown. Often as I shopped for groceries I would see a tall, thin, pale, red-headed young man with a name tag identifying him as the Elder Smith speaking with some of the locals as part of the training he was providing for a series of young Brazilian missionaries. The day after making my arrangement with Bartô, I decided to follow the Elder Smith and his companion at a discreet distance as they too wandered the hills around Viçosa. I had seen them doing this on several of my earlier excursions and this seemed to be the chance to satisfy my curiosity as I pondered how to solve my problem of method. They went from house to house and, in the Brazilian alternative to knocking on a door, stood at the edge of the *quintal* clapping their hands to summon forth the occupants. After a few hours I realized that if this one hundred percent door-to-door approach worked for them, it should work for Bartô and me as well.

Following this "discovery" of the "Mormon method," Bartô and I worked out our plan. After a bit of on-the-job interview training, Bartô and I would split up and visit every household in Prudentes. We would begin with a brief explanation of our purpose and then offer a no-cash-cost package of fertilizer, lime, micronutrients, and the current dry-season and all-season garden seed of each household's choice. The specific types of seeds would be determined by asking which seeds the household preferred. We would also collect a set of household data that included the number of persons and generations in each household, when the first generation of the family had arrived in Prudentes, what were the surnames of the current senior generation, how many children had been born to that senior generation, how many of those children still lived or had survived until they had had children of their own, if anyone from the household worked outside Prudentes and could possibly send home any remittance payments, if anyone in the household had any diseases that might prevent their preparation of a garden, what diseases of all kinds were suffered in the household, and if the household owned any land and, if so, how much.[25]

After completing this interview, we would measure the size of the household's *quintal* garden to estimate the quantities of seed and soil amendments that would be needed to establish dry season gardens throughout the community. We would explain that the only requirements to receive the package were to have at least one seedbed prepared for immediate planting and to have the garden adequately fenced to keep out the chickens that roamed about to feed themselves. We also placed no upper limit on the area of land that could be seeded and further guaranteed each household a minimum of six weeks to prepare their seedbeds. Last, we planned to give everyone frequent reminders of the two simple donor requirements to receive the package as we moved about the community. We also cautioned them that they would receive nothing if the seedbeds were not ready and waiting and the bamboo chicken-proof fences were not in place when we returned.

Our plan to provide fruit tree seedlings was to begin upon delivery of the dry season garden package. We would ask if the household wanted any fruit trees and what kinds they preferred. We also hoped to identify any landowners who would be willing to provide land for the beans-and-trees sharecropping system we hoped to implant.

After working out our plan, I telephoned Little Sebastian from my office at the University. He was disappointed and unhappy that Little Fernando had abandoned the effort, but nonetheless was sufficiently impressed with our plan and its thoroughness to promise us the use of his Volkswagen Brasilia for as long as we needed to deliver the garden package.

Everything seemed finally to have fallen into place.

NOTES

1. World Resources Institute (WRI), *Participatory Rural Appraisal Handbook: Conducting PRAs in Kenya* (New York: World Resources Institute Center for International Development and Environment, 1991), 1.

2. Terry D. Bergdall, *Methods for Active Participation: Experiences in Rural Development from East and Central Africa* (Nairobi: Oxford University Press, 1993), 6.

3. John Bolt, "Christian Obligations: 'The Poor You will always have with You,'" *The Journal of Markets & Morality* 7, no. 2 (Fall 2004): 486–487.

4. ——, "Christian Obligations," 469.

5. Robert Chambers, "The Origins and Practice of Participatory Rural Appraisal," *World Development* 22, no. 7 (July 1994): 953–969.

6. Sebastião Araújo de Oliveira, 1996. *Plano Municipal de Saúde* (Senhora de Oliveira, MG: Copiadora Pirangense, 1996).

7. See note 6 above.

8. See note 6 above.

9. Fernando Silveira Franco,. 1995. *Sistemas Agroflorestais da Zona da Mata de Minas Gerais* (Ph D. dissertation: Departamento de Engenheria Florestal, Universidade Federal de Viçosa, 1995), 18.

10. Instituto Brasileiro de Geografia e Economia (IBGE), *Senso Demográfico de 1990* (Rio de Janeiro: Instituto Brasileiro de Geografia e Economia, 1991).

11. Robert Chambers, *Rural Development: Putting the Last First* (Essex, UK: Longman Scientific and Technical, 1983).

12. Dip Kapoor, "People First: A Guide to Self-Reliant, Participatory Rural Development," *Convergence* 29 no. 3 (September 1996): 44–47.

13. Program for International Development/National Environment Secretariat (PID/NES), *An Introduction to Participatory Rural Appraisal for Rural Resource Management* (Worcester, UK: Clark University Program for International Development and Nairobi: National Environmental Secretariat, Ministry of Environment and Natural Resources, 1989).

14. Emilio Willems, "The Structure of the Brazilian Family," *Social Forces* 31 (September 1953): 343–345.

15. Esdras Borges Costa, "Relações de Família em Cerrado e Retiro," *Sociologia* 17 (July 1955): 132–146.

16. Freyre, "The Patriarchal Basis of Brazilian Society," in *Politics of Change in Latin America,* ed. Joseph Maier and Richard W. Weatherhead (New York: Praeger, 1964), 77–98.

17. Charles Wagley, *An Introduction to Brazil* (revised edition) (New York: Columbia University Press, 1971), 166–185.

18. James P. Spradley, *Participant Observation* (New York: Holt, Rinehart and Winston, 1980). See also Spradley, *The Ethnographic Interview* (New York: Holt, Rinehart and Winston, 1979).

19. See notes 5, 12 and 13 above.

20. Jerome Kirk and Mark L. Miller, *Reliability and Validity in Qualitative Research* (Beverly Hills, CA: Sage Publications, 1986).

21. Susan C. Weller and A. Kimball Romney, *Systematic Data Collection* (Newbury Park, CA: Sage Publications, 1988), 9–20.

22. João Maros Alem and Leda Maria Benevello de Castro, 1987. "Peasant Participation in an Integrated Rural Development Program, Minas Gerais, Brazil," *Research in Rural Sociology and Development* 3 (1987): 43–64. See also Luis Flores Quiros, "The Community Enterprise and Peasant Participation," *Desarrollo en las Americas* 6, no. 3 (September 1974): 77–95.

23. Gilberto Freyre, *The Masters and Slaves: A Study in the Development of Brazilian Civilization*, trans. by Samuel Putnam. New York: Praeger, 1946: 267–268.

24. John M. Cohen and Norman T. Uphoff, "Participation's Place in Rural Development: Seeking Clarity through Specificity," *World Development* 8 no. 3 (March 1980): 213–235. Also see note 12 above.

25. Compare with Ramón López and Alberto Valdés, "Fighting Rural Poverty: New Evidence of the Effects of Education, Demographics, and Access to Land," *Economic Development and Cultural Change* 49, no. 1 (October 2000): 197–211.

Chapter Ten

To Have and Have Not

Within three days of things seeming finally to fall into place, they began to fall apart again. Mid-morning on Saturday, two days before we were to travel to Prudentes, Bartô's common-law wife, Rosemary telephoned the gate guard's station at my apartment to summon me downstairs so she could shout her complaints about Bartô.

"*Ele ficou bêbedo.*" He got drunk. "*Ele perdiu o trabalho dele.*" He lost his job. "*Ele destriu a cadeira.*" He destroyed the chair.

I recognized her complaints as a pre-emptive strike. The worst-case scenario seemed to be the half-day hassle of buying and transporting a chair.

Once at their home on the north side of town, Rosemary continued her tirade. "*Ele fica bêbedo desde tem oito anos de idade.*" He's been drunk since the age of eight. "*Ohla a cadeira!*" Look at the chair! It had a single cracked leg.

"Okay," I told her. "I'll speak with him."

"*Eu mandei ele para cadeia.*" I had him sent to jail.

The situation can always get worse. There was only myself to blame. I had willingly taken on the likely lifetime role of Bartô's *padrão*, and now I had the obligation to bail him out.

Back in the center of town I started walking south toward a part of Viçosa I would have never considered entering after dark. Halfway to the jail I encountered Bartô, bloodshot and bleary-eyed. He greeted me with a hearty smile as though this was no more than a chance meeting during a typical morning constitutional.

"*'Mary te mandou à cadeia só por causa de uma cadeira?*" Mary sent you to jail just because of one chair?

No one called her Rosemary.

He erupted in a rage so crimson his brown skin turned a ruddy purple. Never before had he spent a night, not one night, not a single day, not so much as an hour, not even a second, in jail. Now he would carry this burden for the rest of his life. He was humiliated, all the more so by the fact that the man he had seen as his chance to change his life knew of his disgrace and misfortune. He stopped for a nickel-shot of *cachaça*, the harsh raw cane whiskey that can fully incapacitate a large man for a quarter, and Bartô could not weigh an ounce over one-forty.

It seemed outrageous to me as well, so I joined him for a shot before taking him back to my apartment for a couple of big cups of instant *café Americano*, two sugars for me, four for him.

He talked. I listened, as I had been trained. Any breaks he had, he had made for himself. He had gone to Salvador da Bahia, learned to cook in a fine restaurant, and become a headwaiter on the strength of his ability to please and put at ease *os ricos*, the rich. There he had met Rosemary, taken her in, raised another man's son as his own, and this was how she repaid him.

"*Manda para cadeia*," he spit. He would be a jeweler today, a traditional jeweler from Ouro Prêto, if he had just gotten a single break, just one single break. "*Só um chance*."

"*Olha*." Look, I said. "*Meu chance é seu chance*." My chance is your chance. You will become a jeweler in your own right. I will pay you the capital and you will help me learn. I will buy your rings and pendants for gifts to take back for friends in America and your investment will be guaranteed a quick recovery.

"*Um chance, um chance*," he repeated wistfully. "*Essa é boa palavra Americana*." This is a good American word.

A chance was all Bartô wanted, and a chance was all I had to offer. A chance was all I hoped to bring to Prudentes. A chance was all anyone had a right to expect.[1]

We went back downstairs and together wandered through the center of Viçosa as he talked. What had set him off was a telephone bill for more than he made in month. Except for the basic fee, the charges were comprised of nothing but long distance calls to Rosemary's two sisters in Brasilia. Rosemary had not mentioned that detail. Not only had he cracked the chair leg, he had ripped the telephone out of the wall. After a couple of hours he asked about our upcoming trip to Prudentes. He was careful to get the time and place of our meeting Monday morning to await the University's car and *motorista*. By the time we parted, judging from the bit of bounce back in his step, he seemed to have recovered a good chunk of his self-confidence.

The rest of my weekend was spent in travel preparations and worry. Bartô himself caused me no worry, but Rosemary caused me plenty. It seemed that knowing he might have finally gotten his break had raised a desire in her to push him back down. Perhaps Brazilians have their own version of "red eye disease."

MAKING AN OFFER THE RICH CAN REFUSE

One of the satisfactions of the earlier sampling process in Prudentes was the likelihood that the wealthier households would refuse the garden package Bartô and I had to offer. Only those households appeared to have prepared seedbeds for dry season gardens of their own making. Like the Grameen Bank's micro-lending in Bangladesh, if the research was to identify any single class of non-participants, it would be a plus if they were those households that had no need of what we had to offer.[2]

By the time the late arriving *motorista* dropped us off in front of Little Sebastian's house Monday morning, Bartô was well on his way toward getting liquored up again. Two shots when we gassed up in Piranga and two more as soon as we reached Senhora de Oliveira had him in their grip. Rosemary had taken her sons and boarded a bus for Brasilia. His life was shattered. Luckily there was enough time to get a couple of *cafezinhos* through him before Little Sebastian returned home for lunch. I made sure to keep Little Sebastian upwind from us during the handshakes. Uncertainty flitted across the vainly groomed face of the man who had all small town Brazil had to offer, while a pall of despondency obscured that of the man who had traveled far to have nothing.

When he invited us in to lunch, Little Sebastian was clearly relieved that Bartô excused himself to go call Rosemary. Being used to having others listen to him, Little Sebastian offered advice without stop as he stirred his rice, *feijão*, and cornmeal *angu* into a monochromatic slop before eating it. The idea of self-sufficiency among his social and economic inferiors as a possible motivation was lost on him. He suggested a competition to increase motivation: The best garden would win a bicycle. To me this seemed a recipe both for generating envy and dissuading those who dislike the pressures of competition, but I kept silent.

With lunch finally over, we went back outside where Bartô awaited us. He climbed into the back seat when the Brasilia was brought out. Little Sebastian's world seemed returned to its natural order by this act of self-segregation. He drove us out to Prudentes, stopping first to drop our bags and have what was supposed to be a quick introduction to his in-laws at their home in Bom Successo where we would stay. His mother-in-law, Dona Lucí ignored Bartô as she showed me the home left to her by her father. It stood on posts made of *jacarandá* and was, she claimed, the first "real" house in the valley. To her, the tiny huts of whitewashed, mud-coated sticks called *pau a pique* were no more real than Bartô. Eventually we left and drove up to Boa Vista to begin our work, once again with the constant advice and supervision of the local *padrão*.

I did the first two interviews to show Bartô how they should go, then watched in silence as he did the next five. This seemed more than Little Sebastian could bear to watch. We bid him a glad farewell. I did two more interviews for Bartô to observe, then he conducted the last two in Boa Vista before we walked back at dusk, stopping for him to have another couple of hits of *cachaça* at a little *venda* between Bom Successo and Prudente, the oldest of the fourteen hamlets known collectively as Prudentes.

Beyond the interviews, Bartô had hardly spoken since the *motorista* had picked us up that morning. After dinner we each had a shower, Bartô first. As I read through the eleven interview sheets Bartô walked across the dirt road at the end of the drive to call Rosemary from the only telephone in Prudentes.

Although Bartô's tragedy weighed heavily on my mind, I was encouraged by the first day's data collection. In addition to all the household data, all eleven households had agreed to accept the package, some with considerable enthusiasm. One man had even asked how much of the package they could receive.

"*Quanto maior o quintal, o maior o pacote.*" The bigger the garden, the bigger the package. That seemed to make the questioner very happy.

For the next ten days, including the intervening Sunday, Bartô and I split up and continued the interviews. At the end of this time I had completed 51 interviews, two of which needed later corrections. During the same period Bartô, despite being falling down drunk by mid-afternoon each day and suffering through an unsatisfying long-distance telephone call each evening, had completed 63, four of which later needed some corrections. This experience revealed the value of local people with the emic understanding of their own culture conducting the work of rural assistance, even when working under the most trying of circumstances.

All the households that agreed to accept the package and prepare seedbeds we called Type 0 participants, at least until later experience required a re-designation.

Upon our return to Viçosa, Bartô asked how much he had earned. Of the 630 Cruzadas, he asked for 120, and told me it would be better if I "guarded" the remainder. I invited him to come by for a good meal whenever and as soon as he wanted.

Four days later, he finally came by my apartment. He looked like hell, worn down, troubled, and run through a wringer several times by his family problems and probably a few more days of heavy drinking. I made a pork and okra stew with rice and cabbage for us while he stood on the veranda looking out into the uncertain distance. As the stew simmered we finally talked.

"*Ainda está bebendo?*" Are you still drinking?

"*Não por enquanto*," he answered. Not for the meantime.

He assured me he would help me deliver the garden package when the time came to do so, but for now he needed to get his life back into some kind of order. He asked for another 200 Cruzadas.

The following Monday I headed back to Prudentes alone and completed the remaining 61 household interviews. The first day's results were not exactly duplicated. Of the total of 175 households Bartô and I had interviewed, all but 27 accepted the package. These 27 that rejected the initial offer we called Type 1 non-participants.

Three more accepted conditionally as they were experiencing problems with their water supplies. One newly married couple with a brand new baby hoped to drill a well. Another elderly couple had their electric pump burn out. Their household was one of the few with such a device in all of Prudentes. And the third worried about a contamination of their water supply as a neighbor's flock of chickens had run wild into the nearby stream and all drowned. As these three households had doubts about their water supplies and so had agreed only conditionally, we came to call them Type 2 households. Whether these Type 2 households would be a designation of participant or non-participant households would have to wait until we returned with the garden package. By the time we did return, all three of these households had failed in their attempts to secure usable sources of water, the third of these suffering yet another incident of suicidal chickens.

Based on soil analyses conducted at the University and the crops specified by the 145 households that had accepted the offer without conditions, a package of improved dry season garden seed was put together. It originally included fifteen edibles, two medicinals, and the indicated soil amendments (Table 10.1).

I stopped by Senhora de Oliveira to discuss these promising early results over lunch with Little Sebastian before I returned to Viçosa. His only comment was to recommend that white cabbage be added to the list of edibles. I repeated my earlier description of the theory underlying the research. By relying on what the target population itself had requested; that is, adhering to the emic reality of Prudentes, the participation rate should be maximized. He was unphased, and went into a discussion of the many health benefits of white cabbage. I pointed out that, unlike the fifteen other edibles on the list, white cabbage would not produce viable seeds that could be kept for the next year's garden. White cabbage would be a one-time gift rather than a sustainable op-

Table 10.1. Home Garden Improvement Package

Edibles (in order of preference)	Medicinals
carrot (*Daucus carota*)	wormwood (*Atemesia absinthium*;
beet (*Beta* spp.)	used as an anti-parasitic)
okra (*Hibiscus esculentus*)	St. John's wort (*Hypericum* spp.;
collard (*Brassica oleracea* v. *acephala*)	used as an anti-inflammatory)
eggplant (*Solanum melongena*)	
purple onion (*Allium cepa* var.)	Soil amendments
green onion (*Allium cepa* var.)	4-14-8 NPK fertilizer at 250gm/m^2
green pepper (*Capsicum frutescens* var.)	crushed lime (CaCO$_3$) at 300gm/m^2
broccoli (*Brassica napus* var.)	boron at 0.5gm/m^2
red pepper (*Capsicum frutescens* var.)	
spinach (*Spinacia oleracea*)	
green pea (*Pisum sativum*)	
lettuce (*Lactuca sativa*)	
edible nightshade (*Solanum* sp.)	
watercress (*Nasturtium officinale*)	
white cabbage (*Brassica oleracea* v. *capitata*)	

portunity for all those who put it into their gardens. Now he was phased, but unhappily so.

He stopped mixing his slop. He was not used to having to debate the merits of his opinions. It seemed the discreet thing to do was include white cabbage in the mix when we returned to make good on our offer, so I agreed. He resumed both his mixing and, to re-assert his role as *padrão*, his detailing of the clear health benefits of white cabbage over all other crops in the mix.

As for the 27 households that refused the initial offer of the package, the Type 1 non-participant households, many were obviously (and statistically) in better economic circumstances than the majority in Prudentes. Among these was one household in Barro Branco. The *dona* of the household regarded the offer as a "*grosseira*", a great offense. To her it implied that they were poor, and as she—no mention was made of her husband—owned 51 hectares this was obviously not the case. She also informed me that she was a personal friend of Little Sebastian's wife and would speak to him about what we were doing in Prudentes. Besides, she had her own home in the "*cidade*" of Senhora de Oliveira and her husband continued to live in Barro Branco "only by necessity to oversee the *finca*." Lifting her nose in the air, she concluded, "Here in Brazil we are very civilized."

Maria das Graças, the public health agent, said she was "a difficult woman."

Three other Type 1 households refused to be interviewed at all. At one household in Folha Larga the *dona* opened the door only long enough to say "*Não quero.*" I don't want it. At another in the same hamlet the man of the house stated they "wanted the seeds but not the interview." And in Barro Branco at the third household the *Dona* asserted her distrust of the entire project (*"Estou muito desconfiada"*). This last household was, in effect, also refusing the package for her daughter's household, one newly formed by marriage that had planned to use the parents' garden.

Most of the wealthier Type 1 households proudly provided guided tours of their gardens, showing off how their turned seedbeds were *"bem fôfo,"* well fluffy. One exception was the largest landowner in Castigo do Anta, or Chastisement at the Rock, as it may be literally translated. He owned 26 hectares, but saw no value in accepting the package as "the ants were eating everything." This four-household hamlet sat before a massive red, completely barren, dome-shaped hill deeply furrowed by eroded gullies. Little by little the hill was slumping toward the Ribeirão das Almas, threatening with time to slide into it and close it off, making a lake of the entire valley upstream where all but two other hamlets were situated. It seemed like a perfect opportunity for the beans-and-trees part of our plan, so I made the owner an offer to rehabilitate it at my own expense. He declined, saying he hoped only to sell the land intact so he could leave Prudentes entirely. He had obviously had sufficient chastisement.

In general, many Type 1 non-participant households were wealthier, but not the wealthiest in Prudentes. There were also households of this Type 1 that owned no land at all. Like the household of the distrusting woman's daughter, some of these were households newly formed by recent marriages that intended to use the gardens of their parents. These being somewhat special cases, the Type 1 households were divided into two types; Type 1a, those that refused the offer but were not newly formed, and Type 1b, those that had refused the offer and were newly formed.

Two households declined as they represented absentee landowners and felt no purpose would be served by installing the package. Five other landowning households cited unique reasons for their refusal, including lack of space, lack of time, lack of space and easily accessible water, no interest, and better things to do.

Another frequently cited reason among landowning Type 1a households was the likelihood that an expanded dry-season garden would *"só traga mais gente que pede coisa,"* only bring more people that ask for things.

Also among the Type 1a households were six that were not landless, but owned very small parcels ranging from one hectare down to three *litros*, three sixteenths of a hectare. Most of these minimally landed Type 1a households not only refused the offer, but also refused to answer several of the questions designed to describe the household statistically. Their refusals shared another characteristic. Rather than refuse the offer outright, they responded by saying,

"*Não por enquanto*," not for the meantime. These responses begged repeat visits, but each time they elicited the same three words. These households remained a mystery until two years after the initial part of the research had been completed, but while in Brazil I thought little more about them.

Back in Viçosa I began buying packages of seeds. After completing the soil analyses, I called the small agricultural supply warehouse in Senhora de Oliveira and placed an order for fertilizer, lime, and a boron micronutrient compound. All that was left to was to wait until the households in Boa Vista had six weeks to prepare their seedbeds, and hope Bartô would live up to my first impressions.

During the waiting my hopes were fulfilled. While Rosemary and the children were still in Brasilia, Bartô had remained sober. He held hopes of his own that his sobriety and the capital he had put into some equipment for making jewelry would bring things back together for him.

Just as I had turned to him for insights into the rural Brazilian character, he turned to me for opinions on what sort of jewelry would appeal to people earning more than Brazil's minimum salary. Being of little help in this regard, I turned to Sherry Ann McNett, a young American woman tutoring English in Viçosa and watching my apartment whenever I had to travel. Thus informed, we made a day-trip to Belo Horizonte. He wanted me to go with him to look at jewels, mainly semi-precious stones like amethysts, garnets, tourmalines, aquamarines, and citrons. My only advice was to buy a few small emeralds as well.

On the ride back to Viçosa I became his first paying customer, commissioning a traditional set of emerald earrings and a matching finger ring to give to Ms McNett, as she was such a help to us. Once reassured that the payment for this jewelry would be above and beyond what he was still owed for his first tour in Prudentes, he was his jaunty old self. By the time we were scheduled to return and distribute our garden packages, he had the order ready and was so filled with enthusiasm for the research and its prospect of still more income that it reduced my own worries of what could possibly go wrong for us once back in the realm of Little Sebastian.

"NO ONE IS AUTHORIZED TO USE A HOE"

Our first delivery was a pleasant shock. The man who had asked how much of the package he could receive had expanded his *quintal* garden from 72 square meters to 750. The next six households also had seedbeds ready and waiting, but these were the same size as when we had first measured them or only a few square meters larger.

The eighth household was a different matter. Although the *dona* of the household, a mother of eight, six of whom were still living, had agreed to prepare her garden, she had done nothing, not even delegate one of her children to prepare the garden. This became our first Type 3 non-participant household, one that had agreed to prepare seedbeds but had not done so, despite having six weeks to do no more than turn over a few square meters of soil. This was also the first of what Bartô came to call "*o entrevista horrível*," the horrible interview.

Her reason for failing to prepare was that "it had been so wet."

There had been two brief afternoon showers about three weeks earlier.

Having to ask someone why she has not done what she had agreed to do is never easy, all the more so when she has no good reason. Had her response been something nebulous, the cognitive approach to interviewing[3] could have eventually worked its way to a verifiable answer.[4] But an obviously false response left nowhere to go beyond a set of questions that sooner or later made the lack of veracity too obvious to ignore. "The horrible interview" turned out to be the case in fifteen of an eventual twenty Type 3 non-participant households (Table 10.2).

The most commonly cited reasons for failure to prepare for the package were variations on the theme of inadequate time to prepare. The reasons included three households for which "the time didn't give" (*O tempo não deu*), although only one of these could cite any activity undertaken instead of seedbed preparation: "I was cutting my grandfather's hair." One household claimed no adequate space of time (*Não tem prazo*) for the work, but could cite no alternate activity. And one asserted "*Hoje é de folga*," today is for leisure, and the peculiarly Brazilian linguistic construction, "*Fiquei a-tôa*," I stayed at the intention of doing nothing. This household could also cite no alternate activity. In all five of these cases, the interviewees were approached while sitting at their front doors engaged in no visible activity beyond one household where three of the four members were lying in the grass eating oranges. This idleness was repeatedly observed throughout the 42 to 58 days

Table 10.2. Initial Participant and Non-Participant Households

Type 0 participants	125
Type 1a non-participants	20
Type 1b non-participants	7
Type 2 non-participants	3
Type 3 non-participants	20
Total households in Prudentes	175

between making the offer and delivering the package. Their neighbors verified that this behavior was common in all five households, so the reasons these households cited were considered verifiably false in the first four cases. The second reason offered by the fifth household, staying at the intention to do nothing, at least had the virtue of truthfulness.

Three households cited a lack of anyone to do the work as their reason for failure to prepare a seedbed. In each case there were between one and six young to middle aged, apparently healthy persons seated within the house watching television at the time of the interview. Accordingly, these reasons were considered verifiably false in all three cases. Interviewees in each of these households also stated, "Today is for leisure" and offered no more than a shrug when asked what was done with time on earlier days, although one did offer "*fiquei a-tôa*" as a reason for its failure to prepare a seedbed.

A further three households stated that poor health did not permit, although between one and four individuals in each of these households were observed cutting and splitting fuelwood, carrying heavy loads of bamboo, or clearing the Catholic Church yard of brush. Accordingly, these reasons were considered verifiably false.

Seven households offered unique reasons for their failure to prepare a seedbed. The reasons of two of these households were ultimately verified to be false. One claimed a stream running beside the garden could not be diverted, as it would interrupt their neighbors' water supply, although the other nine households up and down this same stream had done so and this was a commonly observed practice throughout all of Prudentes. The other, with a largely harvested fifteen square meter wet season garden behind the house and at least two teenaged daughters employed by Little Sebastian to work in his local coffee plantations, claimed the truly absurd: *Não mexa com horta. Ninguem é autorizado usar enxada.*" We don't mess with gardens. No one is authorized to use a hoe.

Beyond the seven, two more households had promised to leave their gardens prepared if no one was to be at home, but this was never the case in any of the subsequent scheduled or unscheduled visits. As no reasons could be ascertained, whatever reason might have been offered was by default assumed to be true.

Among these twenty Type 3 non-participant households, some had poor but largely truthful reasons. One stated, "I spent all my time playing football." Another stated that there was no need to prepare now as garden seed could later be "acquired from Little Sebastian." This household also offered all the previously encountered variations on the theme of inadequate time. The male head of a third household worked beyond the community and was encountered only once very late in the research. He stated that no preparations had been made because both his wife and daughter were "*loucas*," crazies; just what Bartô had earlier scribbled on the back of his form during the initial interview. While we were not qualified to make a mental health diagnosis, both women were impossible to engage in any coherent conversation by either Bartô or me. Maria das Graças agreed with the male head of household and found our futile efforts an on-going focus of jokes at my expense for the duration of our time in Prudentes. A fourth household initially stated "*O tempo não deu*," but when engaged in the follow-up questioning ultimately sighed and stated that within the household there was no "*preguisa mesma*," no laziness itself, but rather a "*falta de vontade*," a lack of will. When asked, as the interview method dictated,[5] the male head of this household later stated that the difference between "a lack of will" and "laziness itself" was "*muita pequena*," very small.

The best reason for failing to prepare a seedbed was also the worst. A woman who had lived beside the hearth of her kitchen for the past five years as a result of a lower back injury, could find no one to help, not her neighbors, not even her own children, all of whom at various times after her injury had joined Brazil's rural-to-urban exodus and now lived in the *favelas* of Belo Horizonte. Only by allowing someone to use three *litros* of cropland she owned did she have any kind of a guarantee that someone would stop by two or three times a weeks to sweep out her filth, bring rice, *feijão*, water, and fuelwood, and be sure she had not died in the meantime. Despite the horror of her situation, her eyes glowed with an apparent sense of peace.

For those with children of their own, a soothing sense of peace is especially needed when one considers the statistical differences between Type 3 nonparticipant households and all others in Prudentes.

CAUSES OR EFFECTS: THE NON-PARTICIPANT HAVE NOTS

The Type 0 participant households were not only the most common in Prudentes, but were statistically indistinguishable from the complete community by any measures of land ownership and remittance potential (Table 10.3) or health and demographics (Table 10.4). The facts that participant households were so indistinguishable from the larger community and that they comprised 71 percent of all households provided one obvious and valuable finding of the research as soon as the dry season garden portion was complete. For rural assistance and development practitioners, the door-to-door approach of the "Mormon method" in maximizing household participation in rural assistance efforts is unparalleled in its effectiveness. This rate of participation was more than twice what I had found in my on-line survey of the literature on rural participation and more than twice what Cutz had found in any other efforts through his survey of the adult literacy participation literature during his research in Guatemala as well.[6]

As had been hoped, Type 1a non-participant households tended to be wealthier than most in Prudentes. They featured a greater probability of owning land, a greater average area of land owned, a larger average garden size, and a greater potential for receipt of remittance payments from a household member living beyond the community (Table 10.3). By all these measures, Type 1a non-participant households exceeded the same measures found among their neighbors. Like the Grameen Bank, this research was able to avoid a waste of resources on the have classes able to acquire them by their own economic means.[7]

While Type 1b households appeared in need of the assistance offered in this work, the door-to-door approach was also able to avoid a waste of resources on those households already able to acquire them through familial ties.

By contrast, Type 3 non-participant households tended to be the poorest of the poor in Prudentes. While their probability of owning land was about two-thirds that of the Type 0 participant households, this was not statistically different. However, the area of land owned was highly significantly less, and the difference in garden area was also noteworthy. There was no difference in the probability of remittance payments; in fact, these probabilities were virtually identical.

In health and demographic terms, Type 3 households presented the most disturbing picture (Table 10.4). While not significantly different, Type 3

Table 10.3. Measures of Household Wealth

Unit of Analysis (n)	Probability of Ownership	Land Area Owned	Area of Housegarden	Probability of Remittances
Total Community (175)	.36	77.6L	120.7m^2	.40
Type 0 participants (125)	.36	84.6L	114.5m^2	.39
Type 1a non-participants (20)	.75[a]	164.6L[c]	320.8m^{2b}	.63[c]
Type 1b non-participants (7)	.00[a]	0.0L[a]	3.4m^{2a}	.14
Type 2 non-participants (3)	.67[b]	6.7L[a]	28.3m^{2b}	.00[b]
Type 3 non-participants (20)	.25	3.1L[a]	74.8m^{2c}	.40

Note: 1 hectare = 16L (*litros*)

When compared by Wilcoxon sign tests to Type 0 participant households, except for Probability of Remittances for which a t-test was used
[a]Indicates highly significant statistical difference (P $\leq$ 0.01)
[b]Indicates significant statistical difference (P $\leq$ 0.05)
[c]Indicates noteworthy statistical difference (P $\leq$ 0.10)

Table 10.4. Measures of Household Demographics and Health

Unit of Analysis (n)	Household Membership	Household Fertility	Household Mortality	Medical Limitations
Total community (175)	4.90	4.91	0.85	1.01
Type 0 participants (125)	5.36	5.03	0.70	1.04
Type 1a non-participants (20)	2.69[a]	4.54	1.00	0.63[c]
Type 1b non-participants (7)	3.14[a]	1.71[a]	0.57	0.85
Type 2 non-participants (3)	2.80[a]	2.00[b]	0.67	1.00
Type 3 non-participants (20)	4.50[b]	5.85	1.75[b]	1.05

When compared by t-test to Type 0 participant households

[a]Indicates highly significant statistical difference (P $\leq$ 0.01)
[b]Indicates significant statistical difference (P $\leq$ 0.05)
[c]Indicates noteworthy statistical difference (P $\leq$ 0.10)

households averaged almost one full child more in fertility than their participant neighbors (5.85 *versus* 5.03). Nonetheless, household membership was at a lower level, primarily due to the Type 3 households' significantly higher level of pre-reproductive mortality (1.75 *versus* 0.70). Neither self-reported medical conditions nor any other demographic measures, including the number of generations living within the household (not presented here), an analog of average age of those within the household, showed any statistical differences from Type 0 participant households.

Type 3 non-participant households, despite their expressed wishes to receive the garden package and their agreement to prepare seedbeds for it, were all unprepared. Despite their lack of preparation, most of these households nonetheless attempted to receive the package with promises of future preparation and verifiably false reasons to justify my or Bartô's return at a future date. With few exceptions, the same Type 3 households that offered such promises and verifiably false excuses became quite adamant and agitated in these attempts and often accused me, Bartô, or the both us of greed or corruption when denied the package.

The specific hypotheses guiding the quantitative portion of the research encountered a mixed record of acceptance and rejection. This record indicated that both categories of Type 1 non-participant households were quite different from Type 0 participant households in that they had much less need for the garden package. That difference of less apparent need was most clearly reflected for Type 1a households by almost all of the statistical measures.

By these same statistics, Type 1b households appeared to have a much greater, perhaps even the greatest, need for the package, but this was a misleading statistical artifact of the youth of these newly formed households. Type 1b households became non-participants by virtue of having arranged the use of the home garden of a parent or other relative who, in five of the seven cases belonged to a Type 1a household. A lack of participation by these Type 1 households with less need presented no troubling questions.

The three Type 2 non-participant households had fewer means to rely upon (Table 10.3), but from the demographic and health statistics (Table 10.4) less need for any assistance. If the requirement of having prepared seedbeds is considered by itself and the households' refusal of the package when it arrived is ignored, the two with seedbeds ready were generally similar to the Type 0 participant households. The one without a seedbed ready, having failed in its effort at well drilling, had had to rely on a parent's garden and was statistically indistinguishable from the other Type 1b households.

Type 3 non-participant households were a very different matter. These households supported the rejection of several of the hypotheses of no difference between non-participant and participant households, especially those indicating their greater need for a fuller and more reliable food supply. Their marginally lower likelihood of owning land combined with significantly smaller landholdings (Table 10.3) and greater household mortality (Table 10.4) together indicated the greatest need of any household Type to receive the package. Compared to all other Types, these Type 3 households suffered the loss of more of their children before those children went on to have children of their own. Nonetheless, these households failed to make any preparations for a no-cash-cost, minimal labor, broad time-window improvement in the security and material quality of their lives. Whether their poverty created this lack of motivation or the lack of motivation has resulted in the poverty, the failure to prepare raises troubling questions.

Despite the greater long-term need indicated by mortality and the apparent lack of greater age or health deterrents to the ability to meet the need, Type 3 households nonetheless failed to make use of an opportunity they all consistently, insistently, and often adamantly claimed to want. This finding makes the question of what happens to the poorest of the poor all the more troubling, even without resolving questions of cause and effect.

If non-participation among these households indicates any causality of this greater mortality, then the ultimate cause of the mortality is the failure to make use of opportunities, even when those opportunities have been requested and required no cash, no rush, no special skills, no resource they lacked, and only minimal inputs of labor. If the lack of motivation to participate is the social or psychological effect of the mortality, then this situation threatens to become a self-reinforcing feedback loop that potentially leads to the ultimate extinction of a family's genetic lineage. Attributing such a feedback loop, as does Hewitt, to a "person's conception of self," their "social or personal identities," or even "low self-esteem" may describe the phenomenon,[8] but suggests no way to interrupt it, much less get the garden planted. The case of the Type 0 participant household that expanded its garden 72 to 750 square meters, and had lost six of fourteen children, also stands as a powerful counter-argument to such rationalizations.

In either case, the failure of Type 3 non-participant households to assume responsibility for themselves suggests the contention that "rural people can be agents of their own development"[9] is hardly universal. It ignores the lessons of history regarding what leads to development[10] while at the same time supporting Hardin's "case against helping the poor."[11] If these Type 3 households continue to fail to make use of an undeniable opportunity to avoid or prepare for both insecurity and known difficulties in the future, then to intervene to provide goods or services for them only reinforces their strategy of non-participation in their own fate. Such intervention also denies them the opportunity to learn from the experience of seeing their neighbors receive what could have also been theirs, and perhaps even from hearing their neighbors' inquiring reminders of the non-participant's missed opportunity when they or, more commonly, one of their children comes to ask those neighbors for food. And even if their intended use of the package components was not in their gardens, but rather for later sale, trade, or other purpose, this does not change the fact that these households clearly expected to receive something for nothing. To argue that potential beneficiaries of rural assistance need not respect arbitrary donor rules as long as no third party is harmed is to present an objective argument that such persons should in fact receive something for nothing. It is also an argument for a definition of development as dependence on the charity of strangers. The question is not whether or not these persons deserve assistance, but whether or not they will in fact act as agents of *their own development*. This research suggests that at least some of the poorest of the poor will not.

Lastly, to assert, as does Hewitt, that households in some societies choose, either actively or by default, not to participate in emically relevant opportunities to better their quality of life because they have a different view of time, lack self-esteem, or don't believe they can control their fate[12] is to miss the point. Views of time, self and fate that let such opportunities pass by are maladaptive, whatever their source or origin, and should not be encouraged by providing something for nothing. Without such encouragement of non-participation, perhaps a change in behavior can be wrought so that these persons will learn from their experience and act as agents of their own development the next time a needed opportunity presents itself. Otherwise, the troubling question remains. What is to become of these people?

NOTES

1. John Bolt, "Christian Obligations: 'The Poor You will always have with You,'" *The Journal of Markets & Morality* 7, no. 2 (Fall 2004): 469.

2. Abu N.M. Wahid, "The Socioeconomic Conditions of Bangladesh and the Evolution of the Grameen Bank," in *The Grameen Bank: Poverty Relief in Bangladesh,* ed. Abu N.M. Wahid (Boulder, CO: Westview Press, Inc., 1979), 1–8.

3. Susan C. Weller and A. Kimball Romney, *Systematic Data Collection* (Newbury Park, CA: Sage Publications, 1988).

4. Jerome Kirk and Mark L. Miller, *Reliability and Validity in Qualitative Research* (Beverly Hills: Sage Publications, 1986).

5. James P. Spradley, *The Ethnographic Interview* (New York: Holt, Rinehart and Winston, 1979).

6. Germán Cutz, *Reasons for Non-Participation of Adults in Rural Literacy Programs in Western Guatemala* (Ed.D. dissertation, Muncie, IN: Department of Adult Education, Teacher's College, Ball State University, 1997), 41–42.

7. See note 2 above.

8. J.P. Hewitt, 1997. *Self and Society: A Symbolic Interactionist Social Psychology* (Boston: Allyn and Bacon, 1997), 96–106.

9. Terry D. Bergdall, *Methods for Active Participation: Experiences in Rural Development from East and Central Africa* (Nairobi: Oxford University Press, 1993), 6.

10. Rondo Cameron, 1967. "Economic Development: Some Lessons from History," *American Economic Review* 57, no. 2 (May 1967), 312–324.

11. Garrett Hardin, "Lifeboat Ethics: The Case Against Helping the Poor," *Psychology Today* 8, no. 4 (September 1974): 38–40.

12. See note 8 above.

Chapter Eleven

"The Poor You will Always have with You"

Unlike the research done a decade earlier in China, for the first couple of years after my return to the United States romanticism worked against me whenever this work from Brazil was presented at conferences or submitted for publication. At its first presentation before the 8th International Symposium on Society and Resource Management in 2000[1] the work nearly generated a riot. A few minutes before I was scheduled to speak, the two-dozen or so chairs in assigned classroom at Western Washington University in Bellingham were all taken and even more people stood against the walls and in the doorway. Judging from the number of people who had approached me before the presentation, many of the resource-focused social scientists now in attendance had a few years earlier been enamored of the China research[2] and its documentation of the detailed validity of the indigenous knowledge held by the villagers in Lijiayang and Linfengkeng. Once again, they were looking forward to further confirmation of their neo-racist preconceptions of the "traditional ecological knowledge and wisdom"[3] within non-western societies. They were in for a shock.

Everything went well until the presentation got to the Type 3 non-participant households. The high rate of overall participation in the dry season garden portion of the work, the self-exclusion of the wealthier Type 1a non-participants, and even the self-exclusion of the newly formed Type 1b non-participant households all met with admiring smiles. The necessity to "fire the graduate students" and replace them with Bartô, a "person of color" kept down by the racism of Brazilian society, drew especially approving nods and giggles. But when the statistics revealed the Type 3 non-participants to be the poorest of the poor in Prudentes and the quotes documented the lack of truthfulness among these households,[4] the smiling faces were transformed into biblically wrathful countenances. People screamed at me. Others shook their fists. In the minds of these social scientists the ultimate crime, the unforgivable sin of "blaming the victims" had been willfully perpetrated right before their disbelieving eyes. For the remaining day-and-a-half of the conference, I was a non-person. Those who earlier had altered their paths to speak to me now scowled from a distance or studiously avoided any eye contact if they could not find alternate routes away from me. The committee of referees for the 9th Symposium rejected a proposed follow-up presentation incorporating additional data collected in 2001. They had heard enough.

Editors of what should have been interested scholarly journals were no kinder. Instead of the normally terse two or three sentences informing an author of the rejection of a submission, these went for page after page. For example, Deborah Eade, editor of Oxfam's *Development in Practice*, went on at length about her own work in Central America, describing how non-participation "was often because of bad experiences in the past—for instance, with priests who threatened them with excommunication if they participated in land seizures, or with *orejas* (spies) who reported them to the military authorities."[5] Never mind that a no-cost garden package was infinitely less volatile than a land seizure or that every household's new dry-season garden, or lack of one, could be easily spied upon from the dirt roads and paths of Prudentes. By the third page Ms Eade opined, "Suppose the package had been given to the Type 3 non-participants. Some of them might, in the end, have done something about preparing a seedbed. Is there any reason, in principle, why beneficiaries should always respect arbitrary—albeit sensible—donor rules, provided that transgressing those rules does not harm any third party?"[6]

Other editors were no less loquacious in detailing their denunciations of the work. Still others seemed to go out of their way to misunderstand what had been written. Some even went so far as to return the computer disks with pinched or broken slide plates to render the writing they contained inaccessible for any timesaving revisions.

During a subsequent telephone conversation, Bartô asked, "*O que é tão misterioso á esta gente?*" What's so mysterious to these people? He found the comments about possibly evil priests particularly ridiculous, noting how the itinerant priest in Bom Successo, Dona Lucí, and her sister, the lay *ministro*, had all encouraged preparation of seedbeds during Mass. At that point he revealed the irreplaceable value of a local's emic understanding.

"*Todos os Tipos 3 são Católicos. Só os crentes não têm este tipo de não-participantes.*" All the Type 3s are Catholics. Only the believers have none of these types of non-participants.

Having chosen Prudentes because of its poverty and lingering traditional rural characteristics specifically to avoid the potentially conflating effects of the evangelical transformation occurring in Brazil, I had ignored the matter of religious adherence throughout the work. The small Pentecostal church between Bom Successo and Prudente, the *Congregação do Brasil*, served perhaps only a dozen households in the valley and served me as nothing more than a landmark.

I asked Bartô to return to Prudentes, attend services at each church, and try to learn which households were represented at each. Once his travel money and color-coded data summary of all 175 households had arrived, he set off for three consecutive Sundays and was able to answer the question that had troubled me since I had left Brazil: What is to become of these people?

THE MORAL HAZARD OF "CHRISTIAN OBLIGATIONS"

During my stay in Viçosa in 1999, after an absence of 21 years, one of the striking differences in the town could be observed on Sundays. In the late 1970s the town plaza was filled from mid-morning until late in the evening with people promenading with their families, boyfriends or girlfriends, or in small same-sex groups (the girls circling the plaza clockwise, the boys circling counter-clockwise) as they waited to attend one of the several Masses held at the Catholic Church that dominated the center of town. Similar crowds had been common on the evenings of weekday Masses as well. However, in 1999 the picture was very much different. While some people might be shopping or perusing the temporary stalls of vendors, the crowds were much smaller and the only people who were regular attendees of less frequent Sunday Masses were elderly women escorted by their granddaughters.

In 1999, much larger crowds on the side of the plaza opposite the Catholic Church could be found on Sundays, but not promenading. These people were packed into what had been the *Cine Minas* movie theater in the late 1970s. Apparently the Portuguese subtitled Italian westerns had not been a sustainable business model, as by 1999 the theater had become a 24-hour seven-day-a-week *Templo Evangélico*. This evangelical temple featured several charismatic preachers, much singing and clapping, and large crowds every night of the week. On-going daily morning and afternoon services and prayer sessions drew several dozen attendees as well. In fact, when I arrived at the plaza every morning at six for breakfast, a dozen or more people in each of two or three small prayer groups would always be inside.

In 1999 in Prudentes, as in the rest of Brazil, Catholicism was still the dominant faith.[7] In 2001 when Bartô first returned, members of at least 122 households were represented at the Sunday Mass and a half-dozen more, all Type

1a households, at Masses "in the city" of Senhora de Oliveira. Also in Prudentes, as in the rest of Brazil, Pentecostalism had arrived by 2001 and included at least thirteen households. By Bartô's second return visit in 2003, with a net increase of only three households in all of Prudentes, no more than 110 households were represented at the local Catholic Church, only four of the original six attending Masses in Senhora de Oliveira, but at least 22 at the local Pentecostal Church, and at least six more at a small local *Templo Evangélico* formed some time after the initial 1999 field season.

While all twenty Type 3 non-participants were among the 122 nominally Catholic households, most Catholic households had accepted the package. Readiness to seize the opportunity presented by the research to reduce future dependence on assistance was the rule rather than the exception among the households of this faith.

Bartô's follow-up visits found that at least sixteen of the twenty Type 3 households had "solved" their 1999 non-participation by repeated visits (usually by the households' children) to ask for food from one or more of five Type 0 participant households. The gentleman from the Type 3 Catholic household that had declined to prepare any seedbeds as he could *"pego de Tiaozinho"* was among those sixteen several times. These five Type 0 participant households, what we now called the super participants, were all prominent organizers or financial supporters of the local Catholic Church (Table 11.1). The visits of their neighboring Type 3 households had been anticipated by these five households. In fact, these five households had arranged to prepare what were measured to be the first, second, third, fifth, and sixth largest gardens specifically to be able to satisfy these requests.

Table 11.1. **Revised Measures of Household Wealth**

Unit of Analysis (n)	Probability of Ownership	Land Area Owned	Area of Housegarden	Probability of Remittances
Total community (175)	.36	77.6L	120.7m^2	.40
Type 0 participants (120)	.34	68.4L	96.4m^2	.35
Super participants (5)	1.00[a]	425.5L[a]	499.4m^2[a]	.60[c]
Type 1a non-participants (20)	.75[a]	164.6L[b]	320.8m^2[b]	.63[c]
Type 1b non-participants (7)	.00[a]	0.0L[a]	3.4m^2[a]	.14
Type 2 non-participants (3)	.67[b]	6.7L[a]	28.3m^2[b]	.00[b]
Type 3 non-participants (20)	.25	3.1L[a]	74.8m^2	.40

Note: 1 hectare = 16 L (*litros*)

When compared by Wilcoxon sign-test to Type 0 participant households
[a]Indicates highly significant statistical difference (P </= 0.01)
[b]Indicates significant statistical difference (P </= 0.05)
[c]Indicates noteworthy statistical difference (P </= 0.10)

The Type 3 non-participant households, correctly anticipating their ability to *"pede coisa"* from the leading Catholic households in Prudentes, recalled the patron-client reciprocal exchange relationships described in Scott's 1975 classic, *The Moral Economy of the Peasant: Rebellion and Subsistence in Southeast Asia.*[8] In this work, Scott described the "moral economy" as one built upon the universal right to survival amid conditions of tight resource availability, including access to land, frequently inadequate food production, especially during lean seasons, and a widespread inability to intensify production.[9] Scott also described how traditional rural life had been dominated by personalized hierarchical social, economic and political relationship between families.[10] These descriptions applied equally well in Prudentes. Also in Prudentes, as in Southeast Asia, the climatic seasonality of the agricultural production system meant a predictable crisis of maximum undernourishment, maximum disease exposure, minimal immunity, and often the imminent arrival of a new child at the beginning of each wet season. However, unlike Southeast Asia, the rural poor of Brazil usually lacked the seemingly inevitable tradition of peasant handicrafts to provide outside sources of income and so, if they did not choose to migrate to the cities in search of cash employment, they often found themselves dependent on the charity of their traditional patrons during these regular seasonal crises. In Prudentes, this meant employment by Little Sebastian or his in-laws, including the two prominent Church ladies, or, as with the sixteen Type 3 non-participant cases, begging from those same traditional patrons whose social standing, particularly within the framework of the local Catholic community, prevented any refusal of these requests. In this way, the moral economy of Catholic Prudentes stood as a reliable reinforcement of the non-participation demonstrated by the community's Type 3 households.

With no verifiable reciprocal exchange beyond Church attendance as the other half of Scott's "moral economy,"[11] at least sixteen of the twenty Type 3 non-participant households had to be regarded as a "parasite class" within Prudentes' Catholic community, and the five super participants' charity as the "moral hazard" that perpetuated it. And in view of the pre-reproductive mortality among the Type 3 non-participant households, the hazard of this charity is not solely moral (Table 11.2).

When asked during the 1999 interviews, all five of the super participant households gave as one reason for expanding their gardens, *"para os outros,"* for the others, but three first volunteered their *"obrigações Cristões,"* their Christian obligations as their main reason. By contrast, all but one of the "in the city" along with other wealthier Catholic Type 1a non-participant households cited the greater likelihood of their poorer neighbors' requests for food as a salient reason their own non-participation. Both arguments reflected

Table 11.2.   Revised Measures of Household Demographics and Health

Unit of Analysis (n)	Household Membership	Household Fertility	Household Mortality	Medical Limitations
Total community (175)	4.90	4.91	0.85	1.01
Type 0 participants (120)	5.38	4.98	0.88	1.06
Super participants (5)	4.50[b]	4.50	0.00[a]	0.60
Type 1a non-participants (20)	2.69[a]	4.54	1.00	0.63
Type 1b non-participants (7)	3.14[a]	1.71[a]	0.57	0.85
Type 2 non-participants (3)	2.80[a]	2.00[b]	0.67	1.00
Type 3 non-participants (20)	4.50[b]	5.85[c]	1.75[b]	1.05

When compared by t-test to Type 0 participant households

[a]Indicates highly significant statistical difference (P $</=$ 0.01)
[b]Indicates significant statistical difference (P $</=$ 0.05)
[c]Indicates noteworthy statistical difference (P $</=$ 0.10)

accurate expectations of the results encountered in the research, but through exactly opposite responses to the research's test instrument.

This all should have been expected. When Little Fernando and the two masters students traveled to Prudentes, each asked their groups of the people attending what was the most important institution in the village.

The response was immediate and unanimous: "The Church."

Little Fernando, "facilitating" the group I observed, asked for another institution.

Not much more thought was needed to arrive at Little Sebastian as a good second choice.

These two clear choices necessitated further facilitation by Little Fernando that revealed the philosophical and intellectual limitations of those who place "the environment" above people and see government as the only acceptable solution to any and all problems. He explained that, while the Church was admittedly an institution, Little Sebastian was not, and besides, what he had in mind was something like a government agency. In fact, what he had in mind was so much like a government agency that it was a government agency.

After some delay, "EMATER," the rural extension agency, was the best guess three or four of the meeting's attendees could come up with, but that answer brought forth mutterings, some directed at Maxwell, the local EMATER agent. That answer also lent the remainder of the community meeting a generally enervating sense of *déjà vu*.

In fact, the Catholic Church had been the institution to see to it that everyone got a fish, and the Pentecostal Church the one to see to it that everyone was expected to learn to fish. And for all his flaws, once he could be ignored, Little Sebastian was the institution that gave each of the other two the chance to fulfill their roles.

EVANGELICAL SELF-SUFFICIENCY

Bartô's 2001 and 2003 visits revealed the absence of a similar Catholic "moral economy" within the growing Evangelical community. In Prudentes, as in much of Brazil, Pentecostalism and the variety of other rapidly growing evangelical allegiances reflect Protestantism's decentralizing tendency, as one faithfully Catholic acquaintance has put it, to "divide like *paramecium*."[12] Such growth is an adaptive and increasingly common response to the pressures and uncertainties of globalization within Brazil's economy and society. Planning for or assertions of self-sufficiency were the common responses among Prudentes' Pentecostal households. The landed among them declined, including those Type 1a non-participants who wanted the seeds but not the interview, who distrusted the entire project, and who "for the meantime" refused to participate. At the same time, landless Pentecostal Type 0 participant households accepted the offer with numerous questions about limits on the garden area eligible, the fertility of the garden crops' seed, the time available before the package's arrival, and so on.

Among the six Pentecostal Type 1a non-participant households, four owned land, indicating a probability of owning land statistically indistinguishable from that of the Catholic Type 1a households. However, those four Type 1a Pentecostal households owned an average of just over four *litros* of land, less than one-fiftieth that owned by the typical landowning Catholic Type 1a household (Table 11.3). Sixteen of the 26 *litros* of the Pentecostal land belonged to one household and included the only patch of irrigated rice in all of Prudentes, a productive use of land certainly possible by many other households that fronted on the Ribeirão das Almas. During Bartô's return visit in 2003, the landed Pente-

Table 11.3. Comparative Measures of Evangelical Household Wealth

Unit of Analysis (n)	Probability of Ownership	Land Area Owned	Area of Housegarden	Probability of Remittances
Type 0 participants (113)	.36	72.6L	98.5m²	.35
Evangelical Type 0 participants (7)	.00ᵃ	0.0L	62.2m2	.43
Super participants (5)	1.00a	425.5La	499.4m²ᵃ	.60ᶜ
Evangelical Type 1a non-participants (6)	.67ᵇ	4.4L	55.0m2	.33
Type 1a non-participants (14)	.79ᵃ	235.1Lᵇ	434.7m²ᵃ	.79ᵇ
Type 3 non-participants (20)	.25	3.1Lᵃ	74.8m²	.40

Note: 1 hectare = 16L (*litros*)

When compared by Wilcoxon sign-test to Type 0 Participant households
ᵃIndicates highly significant statistical difference (P </= 0.01)
ᵇIndicates significant statistical difference (P </= 0.05)
ᶜIndicates noteworthy statistical difference (P </= 0.10)

costal households explained their Type 1a non-participation by asserting their lack of need (Table 11.4), some adding in direct contradiction to Ms Eade's reasoning, *"Si accetamaos seus sementes, talvéz outras casas ficam faltando."* If we accept your seeds, perhaps other households are doing without.

By contrast, Prudentes' Type 3 Catholic non-participants all accepted the offer of the package without any questions or, apparently, any intention to prepare for it. But they had plenty of harsh complaints and accusations when their failure to prepare resulted in no package. While the Type 3 strategy of sending household children to beg may seem to justify super participant Catholic households' "Christian obligations" to expand their gardens, it hardly justifies continuing traditional patron-client relations by, in effect, continuing to give fish to those who have refused to fish for themselves.

Bartô's 2001 and 2003 visits support the self-sufficiency thesis by documenting the concentration of growth of small business activity throughout Prudentes among its small number of Pentecostal households. In 1999 Catholic households owned the local *alembique* (cane distillery), both of two commercial dairy farms, the bigger of two general stores, the bigger (and satellite television equipped) of two bars, the coffee roasting mill, and a commercial truck garden selling into Senhora de Oliveira. In 1999, in addition to the fourth largest garden Bartô and I had planted, Pentecostal households owned the local brick-making operation, the smaller bar and general store, neither of which sold any form of alcohol, and the only irrigated rice field. By 2003, Pentecostal households had added, along with nine previously Catholic Type 0 participant households to their congregation, a new commercial

Table 11.4. Comparative Measures of Evangelical Household Demographics and Health

Unit of Analysis (n)	Household Membership	Household Fertility	Household Mortality	Medical Limitations
Type 0 participants (113)	5.48	5.11	0.86	1.06
Evangelical Type 0 participants (7)	3.86[b]	3.00[b]	1.29	1.00
Super participants (5)	4.50[b]	4.50	0.00[a]	0.60[c]
Evangelical Type 1a non-participants (6)	7.17[b]	3.33[b]	0.50	1.17
Type 1a non-participants (14)	1.93[a]	5.07	0.79	0.43[b]
Type 3 non-participants (20)	4.50[b]	5.85[c]	1.75[b]	1.05

When compared by t-test to all Type 0 Participant households
[a]Indicates highly significant statistical difference (P </= 0.01)
[b]Indicates significant statistical difference (P </= 0.05)
[c]Indicates noteworthy statistical difference (P </= 0.10)

egg-and-chicken farm, two single-truck commercial hauling operations, and three first-time land ownerships, all by purchase from Catholic households. Over the same four years, the Catholic congregation had declined by at least a dozen, two more of the larger landholdings became absentee-owned, one dairy farm sold its herd, and no new businesses were added.[13]

INBREEDING FOR SUCCESS

While Pentecostalism seemed a recipe for self-sufficiency and the "Christian obligations" of the Catholic community an encouragement to Type 3 nonparticipation, only one tradition seemed to guarantee full participation. This phenomenon was revealed by the participation rates found in each separate hamlet (Table 11.5). By sharing labor, materials and information among its have and have not households, only Bateia achieved 100% participation in the project. The residents of Bateia usually explained their reasons for accepting and preparing for the garden package by asking, "Why not? It's an opportunity."

Other hamlets attributed Bateia's 100% participation to its residents being competitive—"If one does something, the others all have to do it, too." With no Pentecostal households and only one regularly attending Catholic household, religious allegiance explained no more of Bateia than class membership, or their neighbors.

Table 11.5. Distribution of Prudentes Household Types

Community	Total Households	Participants		Non-Participants			
		n	%	Type 1a	Type 1b	Type 2	Type 3
Boa Vista	12	9	(75%)				3
Lopes	36	25	(69%)	2	2		7
Assombração	3	2	(67%)			1	
Folha Larga	25	20	(80%)	3	1		1
Inhame	8	5	(63%)	1	1		1
Prudente	16	10	(63%)	2		1	3
Fumal	2	1	(50%)	1			
Bom Successo	9	8	(88%)		1		
Barro Branco	24	15	(63%)	5	1		3
Bateia	16	16	(100%)				
Vieiro	7	5	(71%)			1	1
Castigo do Anta	4	3	(75%)	1			
Trovão	2	1	(50%)	1			
Coimbra	11	5	(45%)	4	1		1
Totals	175	125	(71%)	20	7	3	20

Bateia was best explained by its unique family structure. Although a theoretical maximum of 32 family names was possible within the senior generation of its sixteen households, only eight family names occurred, and just three family names accounted for 24 of the theoretical 32. Marriage within related households has long been common in Brazil,[14] but this was extreme. While competitiveness might be a trait with positive consequences' for Bateia, severe birth defects were a decidedly negative trait of its degree of endogamy. Six of the sixteen households had one generation, and usually more, with members suffering endogamy-related birth defects including autism, mutism, lower body deformity, paralysis, and moderate to profound mental retardation. As if these problems were not enough, chronic alcoholism occurred among the senior male generation of all landowning households, and most others, within the hamlet. With all these factors working against it, Bateia nonetheless provided a local example of the emptiness of most, if not all, of the reasons offered for the Type 3 non-participation in the other hamlets. Bateia also stands as an example of the economic value of family cooperation, collaboration, and cohesion in the face of the stresses of Brazil's globalization.

While inbreeding and non-participation in religious activities may well be the strongest correlates with participation in rural assistance efforts, political and social realities are most unlikely to permit promotion of these characteristics as methods to halt or reverse the disappearance of rural villagers in Brazil or elsewhere. While likely no more acceptable among the secular agencies or among the academics and bureaucrats who are funded by public resources to study and serve the world's rural poor, the promotion of evangelical, especially Pentecostal, Protestantism may at least increase the likelihood that rural people will in fact become the "agents of their own development."[15]

What exactly may be the differences inherent in the Catholic and Pentecostal expressions of the Christian religion that resulted in such great differences in Type 3 non-participation in rural assistance I will leave to scholars of comparative religion, but were Martin Luther alive today and working as a rural economist, the absence among the Protestant households of any intermediaries between those households and their "salvation" would almost certainly be taken into consideration.

Beyond this curious religious element, for future research, it would be useful to derive from this work a testable hypothesis regarding non-participation and the lack of verifiable truthfulness found among Type 3 households regarding donor requirements for participation. Related hypotheses to consider in any such research would focus specifically on Type 3 households' frequency within Brazil's rural-to-urban migration, the full range of means by which Type 3 households acquire the benefits of rural assistance efforts when failing to meet even the most simple donor requirements, including sub-hypotheses regarding the frequency of such households simply doing without the assistance, the frequency of such households requesting the benefits of assistance from their neighbors, and the degree to which such requests do in fact comprise a clientele or non-reciprocating "parasite class" within any local reciprocal exchange or "moral" economy.

If Type 3 non-participation supports the assertion of Saint Matthew that "the poor you will always have with you,"[16] and this is not acceptable to those concerned with the poor, then other biblical aspects of the work Bartô and I pursued in Prudentes certainly should not be ignored. The Proverbs anticipated both our most depressing and our most hopeful findings: "Lazy hands make a man poor, but diligent hands bring wealth."[17] This being the case, if they truly do wish to eliminate poverty and want from the world, then perhaps the world's urban elites, the loudest and most constant advocates of super participation, usually by means of government, should also consider the admonition of the Apostle Paul: "If anyone will not work, let him not eat."[18]

NOTES

1. Paul Chandler, "Non-Participation in Rural Development Assistance in Brazil" (paper presented at the 8th International Symposium on Society and Resource Management, Bellingham, WA, June 17–22, 2000).

2. ——, "Property Rights and Human Carrying Capacity in China" (paper presented at the 6th International Symposium on Society and Resource Management, University Park, PA, May 18–23, 1996).

3. Ecological Society of America, "Traditional Ecological Knowledge and Wisdom," special issue of *Ecological Applications* 10, no. 5 (October 2000), 1249–1355.

4. Paul Chandler and Bartolomeu Romualdo, "Reasons for Non-Participation in Rural Development Assistance in Minas Gerais, Brazil" (paper presented at the 27th Annual Third World Conference, Chicago, March 21–24, 2001).

5. Deborah Eade, editor, *Development in Practice,* editorial reply in reference to DIP 60.00/61.00 (September 19, 2001).

6. See note 5 above.

7. Patrick Johnstone, *Operation World: The Day-to-Day Guide to Praying for the World* (Grand Rapids, MI: Zondervan Publishing House, 1995), 141–142.

8. James C. Scott, *The Moral Economy of the Peasant: Rebellion and Subsistence in Southeast Asia* (New Haven, CT: Yale University Press, 1975). See also A.V. Chayanov, *The Theory of Peasant Economy,* ed. Daniel Thorner, Basile Kerblay, and R.E.F. Smith (Homewood, IL: Richard D. Irwin, for the American Economic Association, 1966; originally published in 1926).

9. Scott, *The Moral Economy of the Peasant*, 13–34.

10. ——, *The Moral Economy of the Peasant*, 157–192.

11. See note 8 above.

12. Stephen Arbogast, "Disconnects between Bishops' 1986 'Economic Justice for All'" (paper and discussion comments presented at Session IIC, International Ecumenical Conference, Loyola University, New Orleans, June 10–13, 2004).

13. Chandler and Romualdo, "Faith-Correlated Responses to Rural Assistance in Brazil," in *Business and Religion: A Clash of Civilizations?* ed. Nicholas Capaldi (M&M Scrivener Press, Salem, MA, 2005, forthcoming).

14. Costa, Esdras Borges, "Relações de Família em Cerrado e Retiro," *Sociologia* 17 (July 1955: 132–146. See also Emilio Willems, "The Structure of the Brazilian Family," *Social Forces* 31, no. 1 (September 1953): 343–345.

15. Terry D. Bergdall, *Methods for Active Participation: Experiences in Rural Development from East and Central Africa* (Nairobi: Oxford University Press, 1993), 6.

16. Matthew 26:11. This and all other verses are taken from the *New International Version* of the Scriptures.

17. Proverbs 10:4.

18. Second Thessalonians 3:10.

Chapter Twelve

To Wait, Perchance to Dream

At this point the reader may be asking, "Hey, what happened to the fruit tree seedlings and the beans-and-trees sharecropping scheme that were supposed to be a part of all this work in Prudentes?" This is not only a valid question, but one that may go far to enlighten the reader as to why Brazil, despite its generous geography and abundance of resources, remains one of the four or five poorest societies in the Americas. The answer begins with the success of the dry season garden portion of the project, passes through Dr. Couto's efforts to have me once again do his job, and ends with Little Sebastian's bid for re-election. The problem was precipitated by my biggest mistake of the entire effort, introducing two men who both owned telephones, Dr. Couto and Little Sebastian.

As noted in Chapter 6, one of the idle pleasures of second languages is pondering absences in vocabulary. A favorite example from Portuguese (and Spanish) is *"esperar"*, a verb translatable into English as either "to expect," "to wait," or "to hope." To the American English-speaker working in Brazil, hope often is needed because to expect is too much and to wait too uncertain. *Esperar* goes far to explain Type 3 non-participation as well as the cliché of "Latin time."

At each household that had expected us to be as good as our word and so accepted and prepared for the seeds and soil amendments Bartô and I delivered in Little Sebastian's Brasilia, we asked the householders which species of fruit trees they would like to have for us to plant a few weeks hence amid or around their gardens. We also searched for landowners willing to let us to use their land to arrange and implement our sharecropping scheme. Every participant household wanted at least a few fruit trees, and two landowners among them consented to grant us access to their land. The two follow-up phases seemed bound for as much success as the initial phase. Accordingly, I arranged more fertilizer and lime from the agricultural supply warehouse in Senhora de Oliveira, contacted the state forest nursery in Viçosa to schedule a selection of the fruit seedlings the people of Prudentes had specified, and arranged for a flatbed truck and *motorista* from the University to carry them to Little Sebastian's coffee nursery south of Senhora de Oliveira. Buoyed by this hopeful expectation, there was little for me to do for a week or so but wait.

Once the day scheduled at the forest nursery arrived, I selected the best examples of the fruit seedlings requested and, as far as the nursery's stock permitted, in roughly the proportions they had been named (Table 12.1). These were set aside so that the next day they could be quickly loaded on to the truck in the cool of the morning hours and transported to Senhora de Oliveira with a minimum of time in the heat of midday. Just before seven o'clock Bartô, an American visiting his fiancée in Viçosa, and I met at the nursery and waited for the truck to arrive. Eight-thirty came and went and all we had done was wait. Bartô borrowed a bicycle and pedaled off to the motor pool. By nine-fifteen he was back. Three *motoristas* and their supervisor had all been sitting around a table drinking coffee and "*batindo o papo*," beating the goiter or gabbing, as the Brazilians like to say. For reasons on par with no one being authorized to use a hoe, they had told him they thought the Americano had decided not to go. Nine-thirty came and there was still no truck. Finally, at ten-fifteen the truck and *motorista* lumbered in. We loaded the seedlings as

Table 12.1. Fruit Seedlings Requested and Acquired

Species (in order of preference)	Number acquired[a]
manga (*Mangifera indica*)	300
goiaba (*Psidium guajava*)	200
laranja campista (*Citrus* sp.)	92
ameixa	
ameixa do brejo (*Drypetes* sp.)	58
ameixa do campo (*Prunus* sp.)	42
jenipapo (*Genipa americana*)	47
araçá	
araçá da praia (*Psidium cattleianum*)	38
araçá doce (*Myrcia* sp.)	28
araçá rei (*Merlierea* sp.)	15
cajá mirim (*Spondias macrocarpa*)	16
abricó de macaco (*Couroupita guianensis*)	44
palmito (*Sabal palmetto*)	35
pau viola (*Citharexylum myrianthum*)	29
pitanga (*Eugenia uniflora*)	26
Total	1040

[a]Except for *manga* and *goiaba*, fewer seedlings than requested were available.

quickly as we could, hosed them down for the journey, and set off through the hills to Senhora de Oliveira.

Two hours later we rolled into the town of Piranga, still 25 kilometers from Little Sebastian's coffee nursery. The *motorista* decided it was necessary to stop for lunch. Eventually the job was done and we returned to Viçosa a half-ton lighter and considerably faster than the lightened load would have justified.

With the fruit seedlings finally in Little Sebastian's nursery south of Senhora de Oliveira, I arranged with Dr. Couto to use the Jeep pick-up that belonged to SIF, the Sociedade de Investigações Florestais. This ostensibly was a research agency and to all appearances a pyramid scheme created by Dr. Couto just before I had come to Viçosa in the Peace Corps. Once again, there was nothing left to do but wait. Bartô worked on jewelry and I gave Ms Mc-Nett a guided tour of Ouro Prêto and Mariana, two of the three most spectacular of Brazil's Cities of Gold. When the day came for Bartô and I to take the Jeep pick-up out to Senhora de Oliveira and begin distributing the fruit seedlings through Prudentes, everything came crashing down. The pick-up was not in Viçosa. I had seen it at the motor pool early the day before, cranked it up, and took it for short drive to make sure it could handle a load over the cobblestones of Senhora de Oliveira and the bare dusty roads of Prudentes. No one at the motor pool could explain with more than a slack-jawed, head-scratching "*não sei.*" Don't know. I had made sure to stay on good terms with the previous week's late-arriving *motorista* precisely to avoid such a problem, but here it was anyway.

I went first to see Dr. Couto, but he was not in the office we shared. Next I went to the office of the Department's director. Without telling their intended users, he had a bad habit of re-arranging and rescheduling the use of vehicles for no other reason than to exercise his authority to re-arrange and reschedule the use of vehicles. As was typical, he was not in his office, so I asked his secretary to call the motor pool to find out if the director had again exercised his idle authority and ask what had become of the vehicle.

"*O,*" she answered, "*Professor Laércio mandou o caminhonette para consertos em Juiz de Fora ontem à tarde.*" Dr. Couto had sent the pick-up 250 kilometers away "for repairs" the previous afternoon.

The local car rental company had no pick-ups. If the fruit seedlings could not be distributed, the seedlings of the *angicos* (*Caesalpina* spp. and *Piptadenia* spp.) needed for the beans-and-trees sharecropping scheme could not be delivered either.

It was all over.

Dr. Couto finally showed up late the next morning. I mentioned the missing pick-up only in the context of finally having some time to relax and show

Ms McNett around São João del Rei, the third City of Gold in Minas Gerais' reigning triumvirate of Baroque architecture. He said the circumstances presented an opportunity to work with him for one of my remaining three-and-a-half weeks toward some "participation of greater importance."

His idea was for me to accompany him north of Belo Horizonte through the Serra do Frio to the steel manufacturers' eucalyptus plantations in Bom Despacho, Diamantina, Itamarandiba, and Grão Mogol to help arrange a few more paying *associados* for SIF. I knew SIF, the University, Brazil, and Dr. Couto well enough to understand what this really meant: Let me show off my pet American and perhaps keep this pyramid from crashing down on me before I retire in a few years.

HOW TO FOLLOW UP AND FAIL

The greatest obstacle to the independence and self-reliance of the poorest of Prudentes' poor were the landowning religious do-gooders of the local Catholic Church. The greatest obstacles to my research and its applied efforts to bring a tangible benefit to the rural poor of Prudentes were also do-gooders, but of an elitist and especially an academic and environmentalist stripe.

The reluctance of the three graduate students to subject themselves to the deprivation and social stigma of the rural village led them to limit their efforts to "saving the environment" and assisting the have classes in having still more. The primary and probably sole beneficiary of their minimal efforts would have been Little Sebastian, one of the *município's* most influential politicians, its largest landowner, and its first college graduate.

Little Sebastian was an obstacle in his own right. His recommendations for a competition for the best garden and the inclusion of white cabbage in the mix of garden crops each had their obvious drawbacks. While Bartô and I were able to dissuade him from inflicting the likely negative effects of awarding any one household the grand prize of a new bicycle, the people of Prudentes were able to demonstrate the irrelevance of the one-shot gift of white cabbage. Of all 125 households given the choice of all eighteen edible and medicinal crops in our garden package, only two households, both wealthy super participants and Little Sebastian's in-laws, had selected the cabbage as part of their mix. Relating this result to him only brought another lengthy disquisition on the health benefits of the plant.

Little Sebastian had other counter-productive ideas. Instead of the fruit tree seedlings we hoped to make the second phase of the project, his recommendation was that we acquire and distribute more productive breeds of chickens to all those households who had prepared coops in which to keep the birds. Beyond the greater difficulties of acquiring chickens rather than fruit seedlings, there was the central problem of the widespread poverty of the people of Prudentes. Cooped up chickens, unlike the scraggly birds that foraged around each household's *quintal*, would have to be fed. As it was already, the vicious, bony dogs some households kept as intruder alarms got the few cooking and table scraps these households had to spare. There would certainly be little or nothing to share with both dogs and chickens. Many households had barely enough to feed the people within them, much less any birds, and certainly not any birds that might require specialized feeds to make use of the potential created through their selective breeding. And this argument did not even include the question of where people living in *pau a pique* huts were going acquire the material to build satisfactory chicken coops. The economic demands of this idea made it all too easy to predict which households would become the non-participants in the second phase of the project. Little Sebastian did not like this counter-argument any more than the ones against the bicycle competition or including white cabbage in the garden mix. To his way of thinking, the dry season gardens Bartô and I installed were not enough to insure his later re-election. But perhaps the fruit seedlings would be, especially if the pick-up Bartô and I needed to distribute the seedlings was off in Juiz de Fora "for repairs."

During his 2001 return visit, in addition to learning what was to become of Prudentes' Type 3 non-participant households, Bartô was able to learn how many Type 0 participant households had managed to collect and store the viable seed from the gardens we had planted and arrange dry season gardens for the two years following our project (120 in the 2000 season and 110 in the 2001 season). Bartô also learned what had happened to the remaining packets of seed and the fruit seedlings we had left in the care of Little Sebastian.

Following Little Fernando's participatory method of calling a community meeting, Little Sebastian once again had arranged for the announcement in Bom Successo's Catholic Church of a follow-up garden project. The villagers of Prudentes were instructed to come to Mass the following Sunday—a few weeks before the upcoming election—and Little Sebastian would be there to hand out seeds to all who wanted them. According to those who spoke with Bartô, only a few people made the request and most of them were members of the Type 3 non-participant households identified through our 1999 efforts. As for the fruit seedlings, it seems they were kept in Little Sebastian's coffee nursery until a month or so before the 2000 election and used as a get-out-the-vote incentive for those households declaring their support for Little Sebastian's return as *prefeito*. His plan was not effective. The fruit seedlings went to only a few households and Little Sebastian lost his bid for re-election, in large part because of how, instead of following the tried and true "Mormon method," he had presumed to conduct himself as *padrão* to those a bit less dependent upon him, required those wishing additional garden seed to come to him, and corrupted the distribution of the seedlings for his own personal aggrandizement.

From this work, it seems the only way to overcome elites is to be rid of them as soon as possible, ignore them whenever possible, and accommodate them when their "contributions" do not adversely impact the effort to be of service to the rural poor.

DEATH AND DISINTEREST

Unlike my earlier work in rural China, the possibility that I might "see something bad" was realized at almost every phase of the work in rural Brazil. For myself, the proximity to Viçosa and the openness of Brazilian society allowed me to avoid petty bureaucratic hold-ups and paranoid obsessions with control as well as a long-term starvation diet, but not to avoid political and academic opportunists. If the work in Brazil was be done effectively, there was also no way to avoid another "something bad," the alternate host pig and cattle dung parasite the locals called *berni*. This creature was a little black-headed, pale yellowish grub I had to dig from my feet, especially from beneath my toe-nails, whenever I could get to clean water and a hot needle. With the parasitic elites, if the "something bad" was not a group of graduate students adding to socio-economic differentiation by "saving the environment," it was local politicians or academics seeking to manipulate my efforts at rural assistance to their own personal advantage. With the rural villagers, if the "something bad" was not disability due to injury, it was disability due to inbreeding. And whenever alcohol was thrown into the mix, there was family dysfunction, in-cestuous rape, violence, or some combination of those and other social ills.

Incidences in Prudentes provided examples of the truism "It's not guns that kill people, it is people that kill people." The first person interviewed in Prudentes, the man who had not participated in the graduate students' participatory community meeting because he had been shot twice in the head—once straight in below his nose and once through-and-through the temple—had survived, but two other men did not. During our first round of interviews, a man had been in his bed when a drunken neighbor wandered into the home and hacked the sleeping man to death with a heavy field hoe. We never learned if the killer was authorized to use the hoe. The local po-lice never learned either, probably because they never came out to Pru-dentes to investigate.

During the weeks we were delivering the garden package, the police also failed to arrive and investigate, much less make an arrest, after another drunken man had entered a neighbor's home, waited for his return, and bashed in his skull with a *pilão de mão*, a large, heavy ironwood pestle used for grinding corn with one end and coffee with the other. The local police did come through Prudentes on a few occasions, but never stopped on their way to Lamim, Rio Espera, Cipotânea, or some other nearby small town where they might drink without the local populace recognizing and putting names to their faces. Even an economically, socially, and politically prominent and morally self-assured citizen like Little Sebastian could muster no more than a tut-tut in passing upon hearing of these killings.

In Brazil, as in China, or any other developed or developing nation I've ever visited, the rural poor do not matter as long as they make no trouble for the nation's elites.

Conclusion

Chapter Thirteen

Why the World's Rural Villages Matter

The people and cultures of the old and new world's rural villages share many attributes. First among these is the central role of the family, both nuclear and extended. In China we have seen family-specific practices within the time-honored *shamu jianzhong* and how knowledge passed within the family from generation to generation has led to sustainable systems of agroforest resource management. In Brazil we have seen how, despite factors that often crush individuals, cooperation within the family has worked to improve the lives of all its members, and also how much more effective the institution of the family is than either outside efforts at rural assistance or organizations working to fulfill "Christian obligations for the others." As the world's rural villages and their traditions of extended families disappear, we can expect our larger societies to suffer the adverse effects of the loss of these otherwise enduring institutions that provide individuals with the support, comfort, and sense of place that give meaning to their lives.

Another characteristic of rural villages and villagers sorely needed in today's urban societies is humility. People of humble circumstances are themselves humble in their dealings with others. Unlike urban elites, especially academic and political elites, rural villagers know what they know, know what they do not know, and never confuse the two. They are all too aware of their limitations and material and experiential deficiencies. In speaking with those they know to be more educated and worldly, rural villagers will apologize for their ignorance as they seek to satisfy their curiosity and need for knowledge. The world's elite can rarely admit their ignorance, and even more rarely apologize for it. More often, urban elites regard their areas of ignorance as being synonymous with those areas' unimportance. This is why today, as education deepens knowledge, it narrows the mind.

A third and perhaps definitive characteristic of rural villages and villagers is their endurance in the face of near absolute powerlessness. The rural villager is almost always poorer, less articulate, less influential, and hence less able to resist the political, social, economic, and environmentalist forces arrayed against him, his family, and his future place in a globalizing world. Ironically, if the unlikely ecological doom so often and with such certainty forecast by the world's environmentalist elites actually were to come to pass, by virtue of their numbers and knowledge, it is rural villager who would be most likely to survive such a global catastrophe. The odors of wood smoke and human-manured fields would be transformed into the sweet fragrances of a prosperous life.

The obvious differences between the rural Chinese and the rural Brazilian village, literally and figuratively on opposite sides of the globe, are meaningless when compared to their common traits of family, humility, and endurance. As the world's rural villages continue to disappear, we can expect these values to disappear along with them.

Among the world's geographically and demographically more sizable countries, a society and culture more different from China than Brazil is hard to imagine, but around the world environmentalist elites are more like each other than like the rest of the people in the countries from which they emerge. This elite is based primarily in the world's universities. The individual cadres of this elite are the faculty and their following of student activists committed, at least rhetorically, to "saving the environment." These cadres can be counted upon to fill the academic and political revival tents every Earth Day whenever their champions, the professional "public interest" activists put in an appearance. Other champions may be found among the saints of the world's public bureaucracies and the more sanctimonious of the world's "progressive" contestants for elective political office, both endlessly "calling for" one or another necessarily imperfect reality to change. Another influential source of both cadres and champions, thankfully not addressed here, arises from within the entertainment and news media, especially among its celebrities. They are all united explicitly by the degree to which they "care about the poor," "care about the environment," "care about social justice," "care about environmental justice," or just "care about" whatever in general. They are further united implicitly by the degree to which they ignore, distain, or seek to control the people who live closest to the rural resource base. Next to the uterine environment, and in both cases except for the people within them, it is the rural environment that most engages their newly global elitist moral "outrage," unifies their statist secularism with a religious sense of mission, and generates the subsequently necessary rhetorical extremism, pseudo-scientific alarmism, and "socially responsible" political activism.

The results appear on a global scale in treaties, conventions, protocols, and endless new bureaucratic institutions that regulate, constrain, and distort the choices available to rural village producers. While these villagers may be contacted briefly through seemingly efficient but selectively effective "participatory approaches," the rural institutions through which villagers liberate and, for better or worse, organize themselves, go widely unnoticed. Where entirely ignoring those institutions is impossible, the visiting elites tolerate them to the extent they will endorse the elites' designs for the future.

As for the academics in particular, the process of writing and defending a scholarly thesis or dissertation is a right of passage in academia that convinces its survivors that they are the exclusive vessels of wisdom, knowledge, beauty, and truth. Academics regard those who have not endured the same process as their inferiors, as incapable of making wise and informed decisions, as objects of pity, patronizing tolerance, contemptible compassion, and nothing more. Whenever the subject of rural people arises, my academic colleagues often opine, "You have to learn how to talk to these people" as the "secret" to working with the rural poor. In truth, there is no secret. Instead, there is a challenge that academics and virtually all other elites can rarely bring themselves to confront: listening. From the perspective of the self-satisfied academic environmentalist *cognoscente*, the poor rural villager is the blissfully destructive *ignorante*.

This attitude is more than mere arrogance. It is a necessary means of cognitive dissonance reduction for those who rarely, if ever, beyond perhaps a few months of summer employment during their teenaged years, have any extended experience at the sort of unrewarding, despised and disrespected physical labor that is the day-to-day life of the rural villager. Were it not for academia and the public bureaucracies, most of those who would become environmentalist academics would be both friendless and, unless functional as petty commercial pencil pushers, unemployable.

Instead of the defensive investment in so much "caring," environmentalist elites need to confront their fears to overcome their cognitive self-loathing and its attendant political detachment and social ineptitude. Academics and the students who become academics need to practice and thereby learn the lesson of the "Mormon method" in helping to serve the rural poor, thereby re-directing any sense of stewardship of the earth to the goal of serving the people who live there. This volume has documented the basic requirement to enter and realize that goal in the rural village: One must live there.

This volume has documented what can be expected in the rural village, and it is not the "simple living" often advocated by the "progressive" environmentalist elite. This volume has also documented the ability of a method widely employed outside of, but shunned by, academia and bureaucracy to learn how the rural poor live, what they want, what they need, what they know, and what they see as solutions to the problems they see as most pressing. Only after the rural village has exercised its relentless physical power to change the individual does the absurdly destructive irrelevance of what academic and associated environmentalist elites believe is important become apparent.

The same logic that leads to the conclusion that "absolute power corrupts absolutely" applies to environmentalist elites, especially the academics, through the aphorism that "a little knowledge is a dangerous thing." In his novel *Cancer Ward*, Russian Nobel laureate Alexandr Solzhenytsin stopped short of the whole truth of this logic when he observed, "Education does not make you smarter." Indeed, education does not make one smarter, but it does make one more dangerous. Ideas wrought from the academic experiences of Marx and Mao brought about the deaths of rural millions. In the developed democracies of the 21st Century, it is the same well-educated academics claiming to speak for voiceless and powerless others that seek to foment speech codes, enforce uniformity of thought, and create their own pocket-sized despotisms, that argue with the most gravity to preserve resources against the rural people who depend upon them. Safely tenured, some go so far as to advocate mass violence against those who disagree with them, or against those who merely work outdoors for a living. The dream of becoming the next Marxist or Maoist muse, this time in the name of the non-voting, non-speaking, non-migrating, always "precious" environment, seems more than many can resist.

The environmentalist elites of academia rarely need worry about the stray colleague advocating rural villagers be allowed to make the decisions regarding the resources to which they live closer and upon which they are more directly dependent than anyone else in the world. Withholding tenure, promotion, and access to the journals through which one must "publish or perish," academics do their best to make sure there are few or, better yet, no such renegades in their midst. And if all else fails, academics' dull, maudlin, and "shared concern," often mistaken for wisdom, can be used to justify the "outrage" of student activists whenever "justice," "the people," and now "the environment" demand they shout down any who dare reason to the contrary.

Political elites dictate the tasks of the bureaucrats and seek to justify through the media both the outright and regulatory dispossession of rural villagers by those bureaucrats in the name of science, the same "environmentally sensitive" academic science they have funded to provide that very justification. Public bureaucrats, like tenured academics, are immune from paying the price of their errors of commission, omission, irrelevance, and indifference; so they are also immune to the learning process possible from those errors. For public bureaucrats like Maxwell or Sargeant Li, inactivity in the office at least provides escape from the risks of making a decision and, better yet, the deprivations of rural village life. As these petty bureaucrats are often the closest things to rural natives with whom academic, political and environmentalist elites speak for any length of time, the elites' continuing characterizations of "the idiocy of village life" may have a valid base in that limited and self-selected sample.

The world's urban environmentalists, despite any rugged backcountry, fly-fishing, or white water excursions gracing their social résumés, shun all but token interactions with rural villagers. The indomitability of rural villagers, especially the well-armed, bluntly individualist American varieties who, as one of my doctoral advisers put it, "wear big boots, drive big pick-ups, shoot up road signs, and hang yellow ribbons on everything," particularly arouses the ire and fear of the environment-saving, symposium-going elitist crowd. If the environmentalist and especially the academic elites were not so influential with the media, as well as with the world's public bureaucracies and cash-dependent politicians, their visions of what should happen in the world's rural environment could be dismissed as the buffoonery of the privileged.

A few commonalities stand out among the exceptions to the generally negative experiences with academics, bureaucrats, politicians, and the other mandarins and *padrões* recounted here. Despite differences in motives and anticipated rewards, and regardless of whether by accident or intent, those elites who allowed into their consideration the material interests of rural villagers were all willing to act as reliable door openers and, at least implicitly, trust to the good judgment of those on the other side to make their own decisions. Admittedly uncertain of the purpose of the research driving my request, Dr. Hsiung nonetheless exercised the courage many others lacked to open the doors of the local outpost of academia in Nanjing as well as those of China's national bureaucracy. Equally unsure of just what exactly might be knocking, Secretary Liu Maosong nonetheless opened the door to Lijiayang, and gave subtle notice well in advance of when it would likely be forced closed again. Perhaps because they were then in their retirement, these two did not allow romantic idylls to obscure the realities and necessities of village life.

An even greater lack of romanticism characterized the door-opening helpfulness of those who worked well as field assistants. While Ye Nan had impressive skills with doors, he was not so talented once inside. Little Fernando and his posse had no talents on either side. Sun Duo, from his experience of exile in Tibet, and Bartô, born a "son of the *campo*," knew firsthand the hardships of rural villages. Rather than just endure, they were creative and productive in drawing on their experience to guide both my work and my adaptation in each village. Much could be gained if such people could become the rule in the urban world's dealings with the rural, but this is not likely to be the case.

Despite what environmentalist and other "progressive" elites seem to believe, rural villagers with little or no education and little or no experience of a broader world are neither stupid nor ignorant of what matters in their lives and futures and the lives and futures of their children and grandchildren. They know enough to understand that what matters in their lives does not matter to the environmentalist elite. They know that those who claim to be working for "the environment" in the name of a greater good are actually working for their own purposes, and those purposes are likely to be for a greater evil when it comes to the rural village.

Rather than sinking into romanticism, the environmentalist elites of the world might learn what the work in China described in these pages has demonstrated. Centralized bureaucracies regularly and for extended periods of time prove themselves incompetent to manage resources for the greater good, much less for the immediate good of world's remaining rural villages. Those who are most competent to manage the world's resources are the people who have spent their lives doing that very task, the people of the rural villages, but only if environmentalist elites recognize their own ignorance and dedicate themselves to defending the property rights the rural villagers need and value for the sake of their posterity. As long as the very notion of private property is anathema to dedicated environmentalists as well as their dependent bureaucrats, academics, and politicians, respect in practice and policy for the property rights of others can be no more than a dream.

Rather than wallowing in their presumed compassion and misplaced love of nature, the world's environmentalist elites might realize the work in Brazil presented here has equally valuable lessons to teach. Individual people, rural people included, make their own choices. If for whatever reason given over to sloth and deceit, rural villagers, at the expense of their own long-term self-reliance and independence, will choose to manipulate the guilt of both local and outside elites to their short-term advantage. If given to industry, rural villagers know best what they need and want to bring about an improvement in their long-term material and spiritual qualities of life, and will choose accordingly. Even those social, political and environmentalist elites who by accident of birth spend at least part of their lives in the midst of rural villagers either know none of this or choose to ignore it. The well educated and politically committed elites who place the environment above the daily comfort and needs of rural people not only fear rural villagers, but wish to make the world's rural domain their own exclusive laboratory and playground, free of the inconveniently resource-dependent rural poor. To this end, policies that drive the rural poor off the land and into the world's cities where they might be rendered more directly dependent on official charity, thus more easily ignored, are commonly presented as being necessary to "protect the environment" from those who need to use it to survive and perhaps even prosper.

More than three decades have passed since the first Earth Day when India's Indira Gandhi spoke truth to the emerging power of first world environmentalism. "Poverty is greatest environmental threat in the world," she asserted. The elites have not listened.

More heed as gone across the Himalayas to the anarchy of the Mao's Red Guards and the ideas that created the repeatedly disastrous efforts to "put the people in charge." But the one idea of that period that may yet have positive relevance and practical merit for today is rarely featured in the planning documents so prized by meeting-loving environmentalist elites. At the beginning of the Great Proletarian Cultural Revolution, Chairman Mao thought that a salutary result might be had if China's elites, excluding himself of course, were "sent down" to the rural villages to tend pigs for a good long while. Today, to me, this still seems as good a way as any for the foxes that believe they know a great many things to learn from the hedgehogs that actually know one great thing. Perhaps after a decade or two in the rural villages, the world's environmentalist elites may finally realize a truth as basic as the rural villager: The wealth of the world is created by those bound to the hearth by the shortest tether.

Bibliography

Alem, João Maros, and Leda Maria Benevello de Castro. "Peasant Participation in an Integrated Rural Development Program, Minas Gerais, Brazil." *Research in Rural Sociology and Development* 3 (1987): 43–64.

Antonil, João Antonio Andreoni. *Cultura e Opulência do Brasil.* 1711. Reprinted by São Paulo: Compania Editora Nacional, 1967.

Arbogast, Stephen. "Disconnects between Bishops' 1986 'Economic Justice for All.'" Paper presented at the International Ecumenical Conference, Loyola University, New Orleans, June 10–13, 2004.

Averill, Stephen. "The Shed People and the Opening of the Yangzi (sic) Highlands," *Modern China* 9, no. 1 (January 1983): 84–126.

Bergad, Laird W. *Slavery and the Demographic and Economic History of Minas Gerais, Brazil, 1720–1888.* Cambridge: Cambridge University Press, 1999.

Bergdall, Terry D. *Methods for Active Participation: Experiences in Rural Development from East and Central Africa.* Nairobi: Oxford University Press, 1993.

Biernacki, Peter, and Dan Waldorf. "Snowball Sampling: Problems and Techniques of Chain Referral Sampling." *Sociological Methods and Research* 10, no. 2 (November 1981): 141–163.

Bloom, Allen. *The Closing of the American Mind.* New York: Simon and Schuster, 1987.

Bolt, John. "Christian Obligations: 'The Poor You will always have with You.'" *The Journal of Markets & Morality* 7, no. 2 (Fall 2004): 467–488.

Borlaug, Norman. "The Green Revolution: For Bread and Peace." *Bulletin of the Atomic Scientists* 27 no. 3 (June, 1971): 6–9, 42–48.

Boserup, Ester. *The Conditions of Agricultural Growth.* New York: Aldine Publishing Company, 1965.

Boxer, C.R. *The Golden Age of Brazil, 1695–1750: Growing Pains of a Colonial Society.* Berkeley: University of California Press, 1962.

Branford, Sue, and Jan Rocha. *Cutting the Wire: The Story of the Landless Movement in Brazil.* London: Latin American Bureau, 2002.

Brown, Lester. *Who Will Feed China? Wake-Up Call for a Small Planet.* New York: W.W. Norton & Company, 1995.

Camargo, José F. de. *Exodo Rural do Brasil.* Rio de Janeiro: Editora Conquista, 1960.

Cameron, Rondo. "Economic Development: Some Lessons from History." *American Economic Review* 57, no. 2 (May 1967): 312–324.

Chambers, Robert. *Rural Development: Putting the Last First.* Essex, UK: Longman Scientific and Technical, 1983.

———. "The Origins and Practice of Participatory Rural Appraisal." *World Development* 22, no. 7 (July 1994): 953–969.

Chandler, Paul. *Ecological Knowledge in a Traditional Agroforest Management System Among Peasants in China.* Ph.D. dissertation, College of Forest Resources, Univ. of Washington, 1990.

———. *"Shamu Jianzhong*: A Traditionally Derived Understanding of Agroforest Sustainability in China." *Journal of Sustainable Forestry* 1, no. 4 (Winter 1994): 1–24.

———. "Adaptive Ecology of Traditionally Derived Agroforestry in China." *Human Ecology* 22, no. 4 (Winter 1994): 415–442.

———. "Property Rights and Human Carrying Capacity in China." Paper presented at the 6th International Symposium on Society and Resource Management, University Park, PA, May 18–23, 1996.

———. "Non-Participation in Rural Development Assistance in Brazil." Paper presented at the 8th International Symposium on Society and Resource Management, Bellingham, WA, June 17–22, 2000.

———. "Food, Fiber, and Fee Simple Ownership in the People's Republic of China. *Journal of Private Enterprise* 19, no. 2 (Spring 2004): 61–85.

Chandler, Paul, and Bartolomeu Romualdo. "Reasons for Non-Participation in Rural Development Assistance in Minas Gerais, Brazil." Paper presented at the 27th Annual Third World Conference, Chicago, March 21–24, 2001.

———. "Faith-Correlated Responses to Rural Assistance in Brazil." In *Business and Religion: A Clash of Civilizations?*, edited by Nicholas Capaldi. Salem, MA: M&M Scrivener Press, 2005, forthcoming.

Chayanov, A.V. *The Theory of Peasant Economy.* Edited and translated by Daniel Thorner, Basile Kerblay, and R.E.F. Smith. Homewood, IL: Richard D. Irwin (for the American Economic Association, originally published in 1926), 1966.

China Woody Plant Flora Committee (CWPFC). *Silvicultural Techniques of China's Main Tree Species.* Beijing: China Forestry Press, 1981 (Chinese).

Christiansen, Flemming, and Zhang Junzuo. "Introduction: The Village Revisited." Pp. 1–21 in *Village Inc.: Chinese Rural Society in the 1990s,* edited by Flemming Christiansen and Zhang Junzuo. Honolulu: University of Hawaii Press, 1998.

Cohen, John M., and Norman T. Uphoff. "Participation's Place in Rural Development: Seeking Clarity through Specificity." *World Development* 8, no. 3 (March 1980): 213–235.

Costa, Esdras Borges. "Relações de Família em Cerrado e Retiro." *Sociologia* 17 (July 1955): 132–146.

Cutz, Germán. *Reasons for Non-Participation of Adults in Rural Literacy Programs in Western Guatemala.* Ed.D dissertation, Department of Adult Education, Teacher's College, Ball State University, 1997.

Cutz, Germán, and Paul Chandler. "Nonparticipation of Mayan Adults in Rural Literacy Programs." *Convergence* 32, no. 1–4 (1999): 54–69.

——. "The Etic-Emic Conflict of Adult Education: Promoting Literacy of Loss of Cultural Identity." *Education as Change* 3, no. 1 (June 1999): 33–46.

——. "Emic-Etic Conflicts as Explanation of Nonparticipation in Adult Education among the Maya of Western Guatemala." *Adult Education Quarterly*. 51, no. 1 (November 2000): 64–75.

Deininger, Klaus, and Songqing Jin. "The Impact of Property Rights on Households' Investments, Risk Coping, and Policy Preferences: Evidence from China." *Economic Development and Cultural Change* 51, no. 4 (July 2003): 851–882.

Dixon, Chris. *Rural Development in the Third World.* London: Routledge, 1990.

Ecological Society of America. "Traditional Ecological Knowledge and Wisdom." Special issue of *Ecological Applications* 10, no. 5 (October 2000): 1249–1355.

Fausto, Boris. *A Concise History of Brazil.* Translated by Arthur Brakel. Cambridge: Cambridge University Press, 1999.

Feng Yushen, Li Xide, and Zhu Kaifu. "Discussion of Some Traditional Experiences in *Shamu* Cutting Afforestation." *Anhui Forest Science and Technology* 3 (July 1980): 12–15 (Chinese).

Flores Quiros, Luis. "The Community Enterprise and Peasant Participation." *Desarrollo en las Americas* 6, no. 3 (September 1974): 77–95.

Forman, Shepard. *The Brazilian Peasantry.* New York: Columbia University Press, 1975.

Franco, Fernando Silveira. *Sistemas Agroflorestais da Zona da Mata de Minas Gerais.* Ph.D. dissertation, Departamento de Engenheria Florestal, Universidade Federal de Viçosa, 1995.

French, David. "The Relationship of Anthropology to Studies in Perception and Cognition." Pp. 388–428 in *Psychology: A Study of a Science*, Vol.6, edited by S. Koch. New York: McGraw-Hill, 1963.

Freyre, Gilberto. *The Masters and Slaves: A Study in the Development of Brazilian Civilization.* Translated by Samuel Putnam. New York: Praeger, 1946.

——. "The Patriarchal Basis of Brazilian Society." Pp. 77–98 in *Politics of Change in Latin America.* Edited and translated by Joseph Maier and Richard W. Weatherhead. New York: Praeger, 1964.

Gladwin, Christina H. "Contributions of Decision-Tree Modeling to a Farming Systems Program." *Human Organization* 42, no. 2 (Summer 1983): 146–157.

——. *Ethnographic Decision Tree Modeling.* Newbury Park, CA: Sage Publications, 1989.

Goad, Jim. *The Redneck Manifesto.* New York: Simon & Schuster, 1997.

Hardin, Garrett. "Lifeboat Ethics: The Case Against Helping the Poor." *Psychology Today* 8, no. 4 (September 1974): 38–40.

Hewitt, J.P. *Self and Society: A Symbolic Interactionist Social Psychology.* Boston: Allyn and Bacon, 1997.

Hochschild, Adam. *Bury the Chains: Prophets and Rebels in the Fight to Free an Empire's Slaves.* New York: Houghton Mifflin, 2005.

Hossain, Mahabub. "The Grameen Bank: Its Origins, Organization, and Management Style." Pp. 9–21 in *The Grameen Bank: Poverty Relief in Bangladesh*, edited by Abu N.M. Wahid. Boulder, CO: Westview Press, Inc., 1993.

Howe, Christopher. "The People's Communes." Pp. 344–346 in *China: Yesterday and Today*, edited Molly Joel Coye, Jon Livingston, and Jean Highland. Toronto: Bantam Books, 1984.

Hunn, Eugene S. "A Measure of the Degree of Correspondence of Folk to Scientific Biological Classification." *American Ethnologist* 2, no. 2 (May 1975): 309–327.

Huo Yingchang. "The Effects on Soil Quality and Tree Growth of Burning, Site Preparation, and Intercropping with *Shamu*." *Guangdong Forest Science and Technology* 4 (October 1975): 7–10 (Chinese).

Instituto Brasileiro de Geografia e Economia (IBGE). *Senso Demográfico de 1990*. Rio de Janeiro: Instituto Brasileiro de Geografia e Economia, 1991.

Jeffrey, David, Frances W. Schaffer, and Polly McRee Brown. "The People's of China." Map insert in *The National Geographic 162, no. 4* (October, 1982).

Jenkins, Philip.*The Next Christendom: The Coming Global Christianity*. Oxford: Oxford University Press, 2003.

Johnstone, Patrick. *Operation World: The Day-to-Day Guide to Praying for the World*. Grand Rapids, MI: Zondervan Publishing House, Grand Rapids, 1995.

Kapoor, Dip. "People First: A Guide to Self-Reliant, Participatory Rural Development." *Convergence* 29, no. 3 (September 1996): 44–47.

King, K.F.S. "The History of Agroforestry." Pp. 3–11 in *Agroforestry: A Decade of Development*, edited by Howard A. Stepfler and P.K. Ramachandran. Nairobi: International Council for Research in Agroforestry, 1987.

Kirk, Jerome, and Mark L. Miller. *Reliability and Validity in Qualitative Research*. Beverly Hills, CA: Sage Publications, 1986.

Lan Taigang. *Modern Evaluation of Certain Traditional Shamu Cultivation Measures*. Master's thesis, Nanjing Forestry University, 1987 (Chinese).

Lang, James. *Portuguese Brazil: The King's Plantation*. New York: Academic Press, 1979.

Lee, Robert G. "Ecologically Effective Social Organization as a Requirement for Sustaining Watershed Ecosystems." Pp. 73–90 in *Watershed Management: Balancing Sustainability and Environmental Change*, edited by Robert J. Naiman. New York: Springer-Verlag, 1992.

Levine, Robert M. *The History of Brazil*. Westport, CT: Greenwood Press, 1999.

Lin Jie. "Research on Site Index and Form of Seedling Established Stands of *Shamu* in Fujian." *Agricultural Science and Technology* 1 (January 1979): 1–24 (Chinese).

Lin Jie, Cheng Pingliu, and Huang Jian'er. "Growth Investigation and Research of High-Yield *Shamu* Forests in Nanping Houxi, Fujian." *Fujian Forestry Institute Study Reports* 1 (April 1984): 9–18 (Chinese).

Liu Honghe and Wei Zuocheng. "Preliminary Analysis of the Causes of Fast Growth in Young Stands of *Shamu*." *Forest Science and Technology* 7 (July 1985): 13–14 (Chinese).

Liu Jingfang and Tong Shuzhen. "Studies on the Stand Density Control Diagram for *Cunninghamia lanceolata*." *Forest Science* 4 (October 1980): 241–251 (Chinese with English abstract).

Lombard-Salmon, Claudine. *Un Exemple d'acculturation Chinoise: la Province du Guizhou au XVIIIème Siècle*. Paris: École Française d'Extrême Orient (Vol. LXXXIV), 1972.

López, Ramón, and Alberto Valdés. "Fighting Rural Poverty: New Evidence of the Effects of Education, Demographics, and Access to Land." *Economic Development and Cultural Change* 49, no. 1 (October 2000): 197–211.

Ludwig, Armin K. *Brazil: A Handbook of Historical Statistics*. Boston: G.K. Hall & Co., 1985.

Lundgren, Allen L. *Tables of Compound-Discount Interest Rate Multipliers for Evaluating Forestry Investments*. USDA Forest Service Research Paper NC-51, St. Paul, MN: North Central Forest Experiment Station, 1971.

Mamdani, Mahmood. *The Myth of Population Control: Family, Caste, and Class in an Indian Village*. New York: Monthly Review Press, 1972.

McGovern, Thomas H., Gerald Bigelow, Thomas Amorosi, and Daniel Russell. "Northern Islands, Human Error, and Environmental Degradation: A View of Social and Ecological Change in the Medieval North Atlantic." *Human Ecology* 16, no. 3 (September 1988): 225–270.

Menzies, Nicholas K. "The History of Forestry in China." Pp. 543–689 in *Science and Civilization in China*, edited by Joseph A. Needham. Cambridge: Cambridge University Press, 1985.

———. *Trees, Fields, and People: The Forests of China from the Seventeenth to the Nineteenth Centuries*. Ph.D. dissertation, University of California—Berkeley, 1988.

———. "Three Hundred Years of *Taungya*: A Sustainable System of Forestry in South China." *Human Ecology* 16, no. 4 (December 1988): 361–376.

Morrison, F.B. *Feeds and Feeding: A Handbook for the Student and Stockman*. Ithaca, NY: Morrison Publishing Co., 1951.

Nesmith, Cathy. "Gender, Trees, and Fuel: Social Forestry in West Bengal, India." *Human Organization* 50, no. 4 (Winter 1991): 337–348.

Oi, Jean C. "Two Decades of Rural Reform in China: An Overview and Assessment." *China Quarterly* 159 (September 1999): 616–628.

Oliveira, Sebastião Araújo de. *Plano Municipal de Saúde*. Senhora de Oliveira, MG: Copiadora Pirangense, 1996.

Parnwell, Mike. *Population Movements and the Third World*. London: Routledge, 1993.

Pike, Kenneth L. "Emic and Etic Standpoints for the Description of Behavior." Pp. 8–28 in *Language in Relation to a Unified Theory for the Structure of Human Behavior*, Part I, edited by Kenneth L. Pike. Glendale, CA: Summer Institute for Linguistics, 1954.

Population Reference Bureau. *2004 World Population Data Sheet*. Washington: Population Reference Bureau, 2004.

Prado, Caio Jr. *Formação do Brasil Contemporâneo Colônia*. São Paulo: Editôra Brasiliense, 1963.

Program for International Development/National Environment Secretariat (PID/NES). *An Introduction to Participatory Rural Appraisal for Rural Resource Management*. Worcester, MA: Program for International Development and Nairobi: National Environmental Secretariat, Ministry of Environment and Natural Resources, 1989.

Prosterman, Roy, and Tim Hanstad. *Legal Impediments to Effective Rural Land Relations in Eastern Europe and Central Asia: A Comparative Perspective*. Technical

Paper no.436, Europe and Central Asia Environmentally and Socially Sustainable Rural Development Series. Washington: World Bank,1999.

Ruan Reiwen and Dou Yongjiang. "Experimental Research of Different Afforestation Densities of *Shamu*". *Forest Science* 4 (October 1981): 370–377 (Chinese).

Schilling, Paulo R. *Brasil de los Latifundistas*. Montevideo: Editorial Diálogo R.S.L., 1967.

Scott, James C. *The Moral Economy of the Peasant: Rebellion and Subsistence in Southeast Asia*. New Haven, CT: Yale University Press, 1975.

Sheng Weitong. "Site Preparation." Pp. 387–403 in *Shamu*, edited by Wu Zhongren. Beijing: Forestry Press, 1984 (Chinese).

Shouning County Agricultural Bureau. *Shouning County Agricultural Divisions*. Fuzhou: Fujian Province Ministry of Agriculture, 1980 (Chinese).

——. *Shouning County Agricultural Divisions*. Fuzhou: Fujian Province Ministry of Agriculture, 1986 (Chinese).

——. *Shouning County Agricultural Divisions*. Fuzhou: Fujian Province Ministry of Agriculture, 1987 (Chinese).

Smith, Edwin, and Geoffrey Grigson. *England*. New York: The Viking Press, 1961.

Snow, Edgar. *Red Star over China*. New York: Modern Library, 1938.

Spradley, James P. *The Ethnographic Interview*. New York: Holt, Rinehart and Winston, 1979.

——. *Participant Observation*. New York: Holt, Rinehart and Winston, 1980.

Sturtevant, William C. "Studies in Ethnoscience." Pp. 99–131 in *Transcultural Studies in Cognition*, edited by A. Kimball Romney and Roy D'andrade. Special publication of *American Anthropologist* 66, no. 3, part 2 (September 1964): 99–131.

Tavares da Sá, Hernane. *The Brazilians: People of Tomorrow*. New York: Praeger, 1947.

Wagley, Charles. *An Introduction to Brazil* (revised edition). New York: Columbia University Press, 1971.

Wahid, Abu N.M. "The Socioeconomic Conditions of Bangladesh and the Evolution of the Grameen Bank." Pp. 1–8 in *The Grameen Bank: Poverty Relief in Bangladesh*, edited by Abu N.M. Wahid. Boulder, CO: Westview Press, Inc., 1993.

Weller, Susan C., and A. Kimball Romney. *Systematic Data Collection*. Newbury Park, CA: Sage Publications, 1988.

Willems, Emílio. "The Structure of the Brazilian Family." *Social Forces* 31, no. 1 (September 1953): 343–345.

Winton, A.L., and K.B. Winton. *The Structure and Composition of Foods, Vol .I: Cereals, Starch, Oil Seeds, Nuts, Oils, Forage Plants*. New York: John Wiley & Sons, Inc., 1932.

Woolcock, Michael J.V. "Learning from Failures in Microfinance: What Unsuccessful Cases tell us about how Group-Based Programs Work." *The American Journal of Economics and Sociology* 58, no. 1 (January 1999): 17–36.

World Resources Institute (WRI). *Participatory Rural Appraisal Handbook: Conducting PRAs in Kenya*. New York: World Resources Institute Center for International Development and Environment, 1991.

Wu Xiangxiang. "A Compendium of Chinese Popular Customs." Pp. 27–30 in *China Historical Collection*, Series 6, Vol.1., edited by Wu Xiangxiang. Taipei: Wenxing Bookshop, 1962 (Chinese).

Wyons, John B., and John E. Gordon. *The Khanna Study: Population Problems in the Rural Punjab.* Cambridge, MA: Harvard University Press, 1971.

Xia Zhennong, ed. *Term Ocean.* Shanghai: Shanghai Dictionary Publisher, 1979 (Chinese).

Yang Hanxi. "*Shamu* Forest Management Research." Pp. 164–175 in *Thirty Years of China's Forestry Technology and Science.* Beijing: China Forestry Science Academy of the Scientific Information Institute, 1979 (Chinese).

Yang Hanxi, Fang Qi, and Qu Qihua. *Shamu Afforestation.* Beijing: China Forestry Press, 1958 (Chinese).

Yu Xintuo. *Shanmu* (sic). Fuzhou: Fujian Science and Technology Press, 1983 (Chinese).

Yu Xintuo and Sun Peiling. "Forest Intercropping." Pp. 431–441 in *Shamu*, edited by Wu Zhongren, Beijing: Forestry Press, 1984 (Chinese).

Zhang Dinghua. "Changes in Soil Physical Properties after Burning the Mountain." *Forest Science and Technology* 5 (May 1985): 20–21 (Chinese).

Zhang Dinghua, Chen Tiancheng and Zhuang Zaiwen. "Investigation of Mixed Forests of *Shamu* and *Wenmu* in Hilly Areas of Southern Fujian." *Forest Science and Technology Journal* 9 (September 1983): 9–15 (Chinese).

Zhang Xianwu, Xu Guanghui, Zhou Xuqing, and Zhou Chonglian. "Repeated Plantations of *Cunninghamia lanceolata* and Toxicisis (sic) of Soil." Pp. 143–151 in *Ecological Studies on Artificial Cunninghamia lanceolata Forests.* Beijing: Institute of Forestry and Pedology, Academia Sinica, 1980 (Chinese with English abstract).

Zhao Yi. "A Summary of the History of Cultivating and Utilizing *Shamu.*" *Sichuan Forest Science* 2 (April 1980): 85–92 (Chinese).

Zhou Chonglian, Xu Guanghui, and Zhang Xianwu. "Effects of Plantation Burning on Soil Micro-organisms." Pp. 160–165 in *Ecological Studies on Artificial Cunninghamia Lanceolata Forests.* Beijing: Institute of Forestry and Pedology, Academia Sinica, 1980 (Chinese with English abstract).

Zinn, Howard A. *A People's History of the United States.* New York: Harper Perennial, 1980.

Index